ORACLE OF DELPHI

PROPHECIES FROM THE ETERNAL PRIESTESS

AUTHOR
Suzy Cherub

ARTIST
Briarly Collyns

ORACLE OF DELPHI

PROPHECIES FROM
THE ETERNAL PRIESTESS

Copyright © 2023 Suzy Cherub
Artwork Copyright © 2023 Briarly Collyns

All rights reserved. Other than for personal use, no part of these cards or this book may be reproduced in any way, in whole or part without the written consent of the copyright holder or publisher. These cards are intended for spiritual and emotional guidance only. They are not intended to replace medical assistance or treatment.

Published by Blue Angel Publishing®
80 Glen Tower Drive, Glen Waverley,
Victoria, Australia 3150
info@blueangelonline.com
www.blueangelonline.com

Edited by Jules Sutherland.
Designed by Sunshine Connelly.

Blue Angel is a registered trademark of Blue Angel Gallery Pty. Ltd.

ISBN: 978-1-922573-75-9

contents

Acknowledgements - 8

The Call of the Oracle - 10

Welcome to the *Oracle of Delphi* - 12

How to Lightwork with your *Oracle of Delphi* - 15

Delphic Card Layouts - 20

Delphic Card Meanings - 32

About the Author - 166

About the Artist - 169

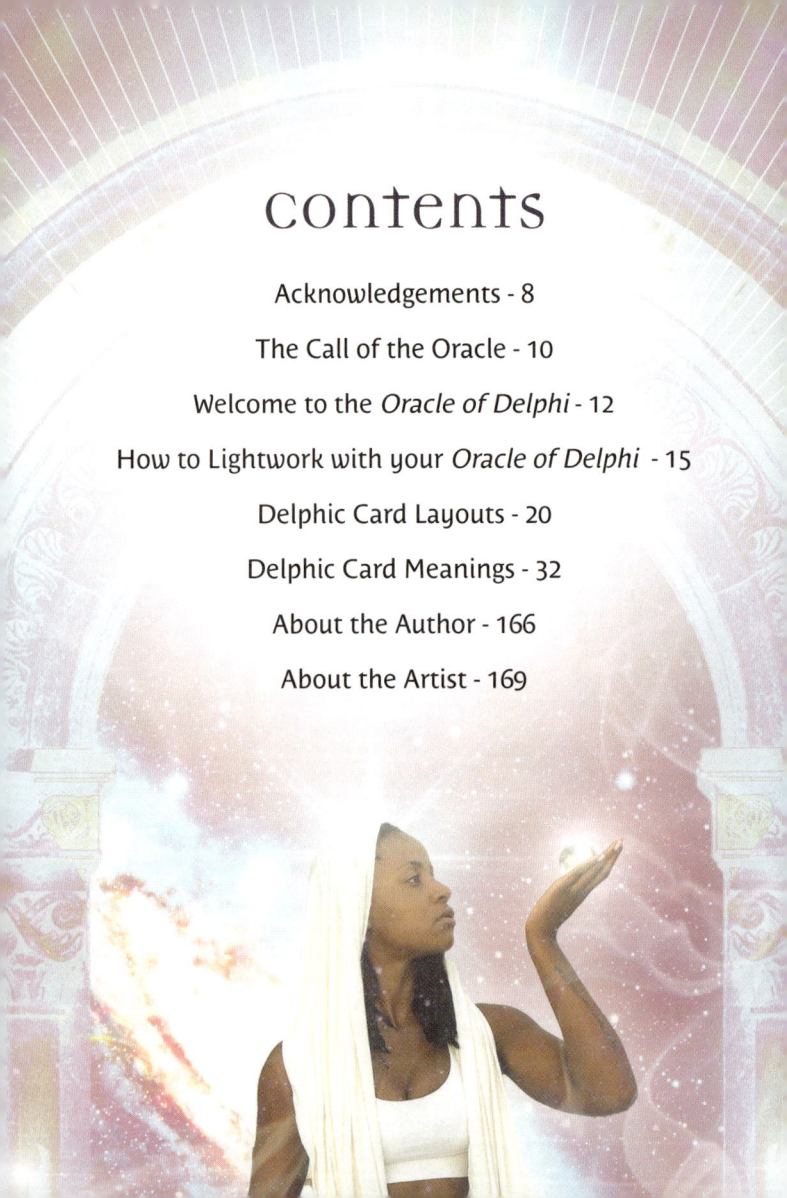

Delphic Card Meanings

1. PRIESTESS - 33
2. ALCHEMIST - 36
3. ARCHER - 39
4. DANCER - 42
5. ORACLE - 45
6. MEDIUM - 48
7. POET - 51
8. MUSICIAN - 54
9. ARTIST - 57
10. GUARDIAN - 60
11. SPIRIT - 63
12. TEMPLE - 66
13. LOVERS - 69
14. SORCERESS - 72
15. ADVOCATE - 75
16. NURTURER - 78
17. AWAKENER - 81
18. SOVEREIGN - 84
19. LIONHEART - 87
20. CARETAKER - 90
21. MESSENGER - 93
22. DEVOTEE - 96
23. CIRCLE - 99
24. MYSTIC - 102
25. SEER - 105
26. EMPATH - 108
27. ENCHANTER - 111
28. SAGE - 114
29. HEALER - 117
30. WAYSHOWER - 120
31. TEACHER - 123
32. LOVEMAKER - 126
33. MAGICMAKER - 129
34. DIVINE - 132
35. ODYSSEY - 135
36. LUMINARY - 138
37. DREAMWEAVER - 141
38. THEATRE - 144
39. SANCTUARY - 147
40. ILLUSIONIST - 150
41. FAITH - 153
42. SEEKER - 156
43. SHAPESHIFTER - 159
44. STRATEGIST - 162

"Know thyself"

Know thyself for you are a miracle of nature.
Surrender and you'll discover a sanctuary of peace
and a flowing spring of knowledge.
Trust in the alchemy of love, for you are a *leading light*,
glowing brightly with the sun, moon and stars.
The flame of wisdom lives in your eternal temple.
Know thyself in harmony with all creation and whisper,

I AM THE ORACLE!

acknowledgements

The soulful quest of divining and co-creating *Oracle of Delphi* has been an honour — one I am grateful for. I'm privileged and so thankful to have journeyed with the seen and unseen dreamweavers of this enchanting creation.

To Briarly, my priestess sister, visionary artist and co-inspirer — *thank you* for going on this enthralling odyssey with me. We danced in euphoric trance, dived deep and created magic together. I'm so in awe of what we have crafted. Thank you for your devotion, insight, creativity and high-spiritedness in summoning the ancient mysteries of the Oracle of Delphi to make this deck relevant, modern and meaningful.

To the Hellenics, temple custodians, spirit guides and upholders of the sacred ways of the Oracle of Delphi in the etheric, historic and present-day realms — *thank you*.

To the past and present oracles, alchemists, artists, poets, musicians, philosophers and lovers of the arts and all things spiritual that colour, brighten and enrich our world — *thank you*.

To the incredibly supportive team at Blue Angel Publishing, who had the foresight to see and back our dream — *thank you*.

To my enduring and caring family, my cup is full to the brim with overflowing love. Tony, Bec, Steven, Noah, Hugo, Matthew, Elise and Pablo — *thank you*.

To my amazing support team, Bec Cuzzillo, Jilanne Holder and Robyn Edwards — *thank you*.

To my soul family, like-minded friends and love-hearted community — *thank you, thank you, thank you!*

Infinite soulful blessings.
In love, wisdom and grace,
SUZY

The call of the oracle

The *Oracle of Delphi* has been calling to me for eons and eons!

She is calling your name too! It's no accident that you have found your way to this oracle. This deck may stir deep-rooted memories of ancient temples and sacred rituals — a remembering that brings you home to your soul wisdom. This spirited awakening will continue to grow as you journey with your deck.

In ancient Greece, an oracle was chosen from the priestesses of the Temple of Apollo at Delphi. These priestesses, or Pythia, were conduits for messages from Apollo. The Pythia, the voice of The Oracle of Delphi, guided the creation of this oracle set.

The Oracle of Delphi first appeared to me when I started my spiritual journey many years ago, calling to me across the luminous veil. She spoke to me of reclaiming the mysteries of the Temple of the Sun and integrating the ancient wisdom of the oracles with New Age spirituality. Her presence was a constant companion as I developed my spiritual practice and learnings of the ancient psychic arts.

When I made my pilgrimage to Greece and visited the temples, my soul-remembering and connection to the Oracle of Delphi deepened. At these historical sites, past life and inherited memories resurfaced to re-initiate me into the rites of the ancient oracles. I felt my intuition expand. She guided me to 'Know thyself' — through reflection, meditation and ritual. This experience amplified my burgeoning thirst for evolutionary growth.

I felt empowered to step onto my priestess path, to hold space and lead spiritual circles, courses, retreats and intuitively create oracle decks. The Oracle of Delphi guided me to open my mind, heart and soul to higher streams of wisdom and ethereal dimensions. She held me while I faced my shadow, healed my inner child and fully committed to my higher purpose of being in service to Spirit and the global community.

The creation of this oracle deck is the culmination of my spiritual journey to date. The final piece of the puzzle fell into place when I was guided to partner up with Briarly—the brilliant and intuitive artist—to bring the deck to life. Through our shared vision, we lightworked in harmony with the Oracle of Delphi and her divine companions to weave their magic and wisdom into both the art and card meanings.

Like she did for me, the Oracle of Delphi will guide you into your heart and shine a light on your shadow to support your healing on every level. You will then be led back out, ready to share your radiant light with the wider world. Clear intuitive insights will become second nature to you.

Through these cards and the messages within, the Oracle of Delphi leads the way for you to embody your mystical powers. She holds space for you to unite with her immense insight, knowledge and intoxicating sacredness. May her priestess mysteries and devotional love crack your heart open to reveal your unique gifts.

welcome to the oracle of Delphi

Breathe deep. When you lose your way, come home to your temple.

— **The Oracle**

Step into the Temple of the Sun and immerse yourself in the wisdom and light of the *Oracle of Delphi*.

The High Priestess of Apollo and Hellenic gods and goddesses hold space for you to unearth your intuitive awareness, sovereignty and creative light.

Each card is encrypted with sacred symbology, alchemical medicine and relevant insights for modern times. The *Oracle of Delphi* invites you to step up, show up and shine! Call forth your desires and intentions. This card set is a master manifestation tool that supports you in aligning with your dreams and ascending to astonishing heights. The seeded messages within these cards will unlock temple doorways, unleash your magical allure and magnetise your desires.

There is both light and shadow within these cards. The sunlight of Apollo and the darkness of Hades have insight and wisdom to share. Spiritual balance ebbs and flows with the shadow of the ego and the light of the soul.

Do not fear the shadow! The seasons of life dance in divine harmony, which means the light of summer and the darkness of winter. There are many lessons and blessings to be found in the shadow.

The *Oracle of Delphi* was created as an intuitive tool for spiritual guidance, awareness and empowerment. However, it is not a replacement for professional advice. Ask for help! When necessary, reach out to a qualified medical specialist or credible helpline for assistance.

Enter the Temple of the Sun

Let's take our souls for a trek up the sacred Mount,
and listen to the magical murmurs of ancient oracles
and modern-day mystics. Arise above the earth temple into the
miracle that you are. You are higher than the colossal rocks on
Mount Parnassus, and more radiant than Apollo's sun.

The Temple of the Sun was the temple dedicated to Apollo at Delphi on Mount Parnassus in ancient Greece. It was one of the most illustrious temples in ancient Greece, honoured as the navel of the world and centre of the earth. "Know thyself!" was inscribed at the gateway of the temple.

In Greek mythology, Zeus located the centre of the world by freeing an eagle from each of its four corners. They met at Delphi and Zeus consecrated the spot with a sacred stone called omphalos, which means 'navel'. The sacred stone was then placed under the protection of Gaia, Goddess of the Earth, and her serpent child, Python.

It is said that Apollo challenged Python to a mighty clash and won. As a reward, he was able to establish his sanctuary at Delphi. Apollo—in the form of a dolphin—guided people from the island of Crete to the scenic haven of Delphi, where they constructed the Temple of the Sun in his honour.

Meet the Oracle of Delphi

The Oracle of Delphi was the High Priestess of the Temple of Apollo. Also known as the Pythia, she served as the oracle of the temple and was renowned for divining the future. She held sacred significance throughout much of the ancient world, with notable delegates from as far as Rome and Egypt journeying to consult the Pythia.

The Pythia was adored, for it was believed that she channelled predictions directly from Apollo himself while immersed in a dreamlike trance. It is said that she would enter a hypnotic state by inhaling fragrant fumes emitted from deep crevices in the earth.

Young, highly educated women of noble birth would train as priestesses of the temple, dedicating their life to sacred service and often living reclusively. The priestess internship included prophecy, alchemy and ritual.

They learned to craft a connection between the natural and spiritual worlds, merging earth and ceremonial magic in their devotional duties. Earth magic engages with natural forces directly, whereas ceremonial magic summons spirits. In their practices, the priestesses used techniques that combined plants, trees, crystals, candles and fragrant smoke with trance meditation, ritual, chanting, dancing and dreamweaving.

This cohort of devoted initiates and trained priestesses aided the Oracle of Delphi with summits and sacred ceremonies. On her passing, the Oracle would announce her successor. They would continue her legacy of divine prophecy. Modern psychics often call on the Oracle of Delphi for intuitive support, as she is a prevalent and highly trusted spirit guide to contemporary mystics.

How to Lightwork with your Oracle of Delphi

Decoding the Cards

To make the most of your ascension journey with the *Oracle of Delphi*, take the time to read and decode the card meanings intuitively.

Each oracle card is like a portal, designed to offer guidance and clarity. Reflecting on each card deepens your understanding of the oracle message and how the meaning and artwork are relevant to your life's journey. It also fosters your spiritual growth and builds your intuitive confidence.

Begin your oracle readings by shuffling the cards while determining an intention, focus or question. You may wish to try one of the card layouts below, create your own or select as many cards as feel right for you in the moment. Trust that your soul light will guide you to the most helpful oracle cards for supportive and empowering guidance.

Contemplate the oracle cards to see beyond the surface-level meanings. The words and images serve only to guide your focus. Notice when symbols, words, colours or pictures leap out to you. Do they have personal significance? Interpret the meaning using all your senses and trust the answers that come.

Gain further insights by energetically connecting with the divine guardian of the card. You may even want to have an interactive conversation with them. Do they have any guidance for you? Be confident in the messages you receive. Focus on how you can use this wisdom to be of devotional service.

Complete every reading with a heartfelt expression of gratitude. "Thank you," is a potent prayer. Say it with real heart: "Thank you, thank you, thank you."

Each Card Includes:

Keywords: Concise clues that lead to more insights. The three keywords on each card act as breadcrumbs for quick, intuitive answers to your spiritual questions, or as a prompt for further introspection.

The Oracle's Prophecy: A succinct, predictive premonition from the Oracle of Delphi herself. She implores you to trust your own intuitive whispers and interpret the most relevant meaning for you.

Chakra: In ancient Sanskrit, the word chakra means 'wheel' and refers to the energy portals in your body. Chakras affect your emotional and physical wellbeing. You are healthiest when your chakras are aligned and balanced. Each oracle card has a corresponding chakra, guiding you to the area of the body most beneficial to focus on.

Talisman: Coming from the ancient Greek word telesema, meaning 'completion' or 'accomplishment', a talisman is an object, often used in spiritual rites, that is said to have mystical powers to protect and heal. The talisman included in each card aligns with the symbology of the oracle meaning, offering a deeper interpretation and activation of the card's magic.

Faith in Action Step: A recommended practical action that you can take to further integrate the message of the card in your life. Faith in action is the willingness to deliberately move toward your dreams with confidence and heartfelt conviction, even when it feels challenging. The action step in each card underpins the oracle meaning with a proactive approach to accomplishing your desires.

Artist Insights: Three powerful downloads from artist, Briarly, that came through as she intuitively crafted the artwork for each card.

The Temple of the Sun Invocation — Blessing Your Deck

Dedicate your *Oracle of Delphi* deck to the highest transmission of eternal wisdom by imbuing it with the golden light of the Sun God, Apollo.

Lovingly cradle the deck in both hands and lift the cards up to Apollo's sunbeams of prophecy, love and artistic creation. Visualise sunshine caressing and blessing the cards for higher service to yourself and others. Soak up the radiant light, inhale it, become present and hold the deck to your third eye, imprinting it with visionary insight.

Declare the following affirmation. As you do so, sense infinite rays of higher consciousness enlightening your soul:

I arise with the everlasting sunlight of love.

Get to know each card intimately by reading and intuitively interpreting the meanings. Becoming acquainted with the card meanings will reinforce your confidence in your intuition, strengthen your sacred powers and unite you with the Oracle of Delphi for deific support.

To expand your intuition, invoke the Oracle using the affirmation below:

I call upon the Oracle of Delphi for higher guidance.

Temple Ritual — The Oracle Devotion

To open, sanctify and infuse your sacred space with potent intention, you may wish to practice this whole body prayer.

Vibrational Preparation

Get yourself into a relaxed or trance-like state by dancing, meditating or listening to high frequency music or nature sounds. Visualise iridescent sunshine and moondust infusing your whole being. Imagine your body vibrating and creating electromagnetic waves that realign you with your higher self and the Divine.

Whole Body Prayer

Stand tall with your feet shoulder-width apart. Take three deep, grounding breaths to balance yourself. Energetically link to Mama Earth and feel her heartbeat pulse up through your spine and chakras, aligning your multi-dimensional bodies.

With your palms facing the hallowed ground below, say with intention:

I AM one with the Earth Mother.

With your hands in the prayer position at your heart centre, smile blissfully and say with real heart:

I AM one with my inner oracle.

Softly close your eyes, bow your head, place your hands in the prayer position at your third eye and say:

I AM one with the Oracle of Delphi.

Reaching up to the sun and moon above, say:

I AM one with my higher self.

With open arms, palms facing upwards, say:

I AM one with universal wisdom.

The Oracle of Delphi Activation — Igniting Your Intuition

Close your eyes and take three mindful breaths. Visualise an ethereal temple glowing brightly before you, encircled by a luminous lilac sea and a veil of magical mist.

The guardian priestess of this sanctuary guides you gracefully up the white quartz steps and through the radiant portal into the temple. When you reach the centre, silver moonbeams shine down to activate your crown chakra. You feel yourself opening to crystal clear guidance.

Imagine bathing in the glistening moonlight as it transmutes any fear, doubt or restrictive beliefs that you've been holding on to. The sparkly moondust brings you to a state of euphoric bliss. As your heart, mind and spirit expand with cosmic wisdom and love, affirm the following:

I call upon Delphic wisdom to harness my innate magic. I devote myself to raising the universal vibration to a higher perspective of soul unity.

Delphic Card Layouts

Use the card layout from the examples below that feels the most fitting for your enquiry. Alternatively, use a spread of your own or let your inner oracle guide the number of cards you choose.

The following layouts each encourage you to invoke (or call on) the energy of a particular archetype or deity. To do this, you can simply tune into the energy you feel this archetype represents for you. Or you might like to seek more information from their relevant card meaning in this guidebook or other sources. You may wish to speak your invocation out loud (e.g., "I call on the Magicmaker to be present here with me, and guide my reading for my highest good.") Alternatively, you can choose to speak or just feel your invocation silently.

ASK THE ORACLE
Ask and you shall receive!

This potent single-card reading offers a swift answer to your question.

- Shuffle the cards.
- Invoke the Oracle of Delphi for priestess support.

- With intention, ask the Oracle a question.
- Nestle the deck close to your heart and sense yourself being infused with a mist of spiritual wisdom.
- Select one card from anywhere in the deck.
- Tune in to the card for intuitive guidance and messages.
- Refer to the guidebook and use your inner wisdom to interpret the meaning.
- You may wish to journal for more in-depth insights to navigate upwards and onwards on your journey.

Temple of the Sun Insights

One step closer... one step at a time... just take that next step!

Card 1: Present Insight
Card 2: Future Insight

Use this potent two-card layout for insight into your present situation and guidance for your immediate future. Both cards are sun-drenched signposts to profound meaning.

- Shuffle the cards.
- Invoke the Sun God, Apollo, for illumination.
- With intention, ask your question.

- Hold the deck up to the light and visualise sunbeams activating the cards.
- Select two cards from anywhere in the deck.
- Place the cards side-by-side, per the diagram.
- Tune in to the Temple of the Sun for clear guidance.
- Refer to the guidebook and use your inner oracle to interpret each card's significance.

ALCHEMIST CARD SPREAD
Pressure turns carbon into diamonds!

Card 1: Healing Insight
Card 2: Transformation Insight

Use this potent two-card layout when you are seeking to heal and transform a situation in your life.

- Shuffle the cards.
- Invoke the Alchemist for transformational guidance.
- With intention, ask your question.
- Uplift the deck and envision darkness transforming into light.
- Select two cards from anywhere in the deck.

- Place the cards side-by-side, per the diagram.
- Tune in to the Alchemist for relevant guidance.
- Refer to the guidebook and use your inner oracle to interpret each card's significance.

Hecate's Crossroads Card Spread
At a crossroads, be ready to rise into the light of love.

Card 1: Moonshadow — Negative consequences
Card 2: Moonlight — Positive consequences
Card 3: Violet Flame — Life lessons and blessings for spiritual growth

Turn to this three-card layout when there is a fork in the road and a choice to be made. There are multiple paths forward — this card spread inspired by the Triple Goddess, Hecate, will help you choose wisely.

- Shuffle the cards.
- Invoke the wise Goddess Hecate for support. She will guide you in the direction of your higher and happier pathway.
- With intention, focus on the decision you seek guidance for.
- Choose one possible path forward as the focus for this card reading.

- Tap the top of the deck with your knuckles and imagine the cards being infused with Hecate's violet flame of transmutation.
- Select three cards from anywhere in the deck.
- Place the cards side by side in the order you choose them, per the diagram.
- Tune in to your inner wisdom for guidance.
- Refer to the guidebook and use your intuition to interpret each card's significance.
- You may also wish to make a list of pros and cons to discern a clear way forward.
- Repeat the sequence for the other options in the decision-making process.

Magicmaker Card Spread
Ask, believe and receive. Be the magic!

Card 1: Summon — Ask for guidance to help you achieve your wishes. This will propel you to the message which is most pertinent to igniting your desires.
Card 2: Wish — Close your eyes and make a wish! Focused intention gives this card meaning more relevance and magical potency.
Card 3: Manifest — Explore the magic of manifestation via the oracle insights and faith in action step on this card.

Turn to this three-card layout when calling in your desires and wishes. Create magic with the guidance of the Oracle. Manifest with all your senses and potent intention.

- Shuffle the cards.
- Invoke the Magicmaker for support. She will guide you in the direction of your wishes.
- Focus on the desire you seek guidance for.
- Tap the top of the deck with your knuckles and imagine the cards being infused with an orb of electric blue light.
- Select three cards from anywhere in the deck.
- Place the cards side by side in the order of choosing, as per the diagram.
- Tune in to your inner magic and intuition for guidance.
- Refer to the guidebook and use your intuition to interpret each card's significance.

ARCHER CARD SPREAD
Focus thyself to achieve mastery!

Card 1: Surrender — Let go!
Card 2: Align — Call In
Card 3: Focus — Pivot
Card 4: Target — Aim

You will hit your mark with the targeted guidance from this four-card layout. It's time for inspired action.

- Shuffle the cards.
- Invoke the Archer for support.
- With intention, ask a question or hold a focus for your reading.
- Tap the top of the deck and imagine an arrow piercing the cards with a ray of golden light.
- Select four cards from anywhere in the deck.
- Lay the cards out in the order they are chosen, as per the diagram.
- Tune in to your inner wisdom for clear guidance.
- Refer to the guidebook and interpret the significance of the cards intuitively.
- Follow the guidance of the cards and you'll shoot right to the heart of your target.

Pandora's Box Insights

As Pandora unleashes ramifications, she catches hope before it can escape.

Card 1: Positive Potential — Seek the **upshots** encrypted in this card.
Card 2: Challenging Potential — Intuit any **red flags** to be aware of moving forward.
Card 3: Immediate Future — Uncover the **after-effects** of your choice.
Card 4: Future Learning — Discover the **lessons** your choice may bring.
Card 5: Future Gifts — Focus on the **blessings** your choice may bring.
Card 6: Osmosis — Engage your mind's eye to scry for visual clues to the **ripple effects** of your choice.
Card 7: Hope — In full faith, seek Pandora's counsel to get clear on your **dreams**.

Pandora teaches us that every action has a consequence, yet regardless of life's repercussions, hope always remains. She advises that being overly cautious can be the greatest danger of all!

"I love you," is inscribed on Pandora's box. Loving intention is the key to opening it.

Use this seven-card layout for insights into the ramifications of following unknown pathways. All cards offer probabilities and profound insights of a potential path.

- Shuffle the cards.
- With your loving intention, invoke Pandora to seek potential implications of your chosen path.
- With intention, ask Pandora your question.
- As you hold the deck, imagine it is Pandora's box and visualise the cards catching alight with insight.
- Select seven cards from anywhere in the deck.
- Place the cards side by side as per the diagram.
- Tap in to your inner reserves of hope for reassuring guidance.
- Refer to the guidebook and use your inner oracle to interpret each card's significance.

Mystic Card Spread

Sensing the mysteries, you followed her moonlight. Flow into the mystique!

Card 1: Past Guidance
Card 2: Present Guidance
Card 3: Future Guidance
Card 4: Potential Outcome
Card 5: Further Past Guidance
Card 6: Further Present Guidance
Card 7: Further Future Guidance
Card 8: Potential Outcome

This eight-card layout provides an expanded view of a situation, sees the bigger picture and provides nuanced insight.

To glean more comprehensive guidance, timeline framework and meaning from your pathfinding prophecies, you may wish to align the top and bottom rows of cards. The mystical temple pillars encourage you to dig deeper for more profound insights. The first vertical pillar (Cards 1 and 5) offers significant guidance about lessons and blessings from a past situation you may be questioning. The second aligned column (Cards 2 and 6) refers to your current situation, offering two oracle portals for accompanying spiritual guidance. The third upright row of (Cards 3 and 7) offers guidance moving forward and hope for the future. The final row (Cards 4 and 8) offers twofold guidance around potential outcomes into the future.

- Shuffle the cards.
- Invoke the Mystic for support.
- Ask a question or have a focus for the reading.
- Tap the top of the deck with your knuckle and energetically cleanse and infuse the cards with ultraviolet light.
- Select eight cards from anywhere in the deck.
- Lay the cards out in the order of choosing, per the diagram.
- Tune in to the entire layout to see how the cards weave together and connect to create different meanings and provide deeper insight into the bigger picture.
- Contemplate the relationships between the cards for more comprehensive messages. Pay particular attention to signs that appear meaningfully related. When you notice repetitive symbols and themes in the cards—such as wings, the infinity sign, etc.—look for their spiritual meanings, as these are often synchronicity signs.
- Refer to the guidebook and use your intuition to interpret each card's significance.

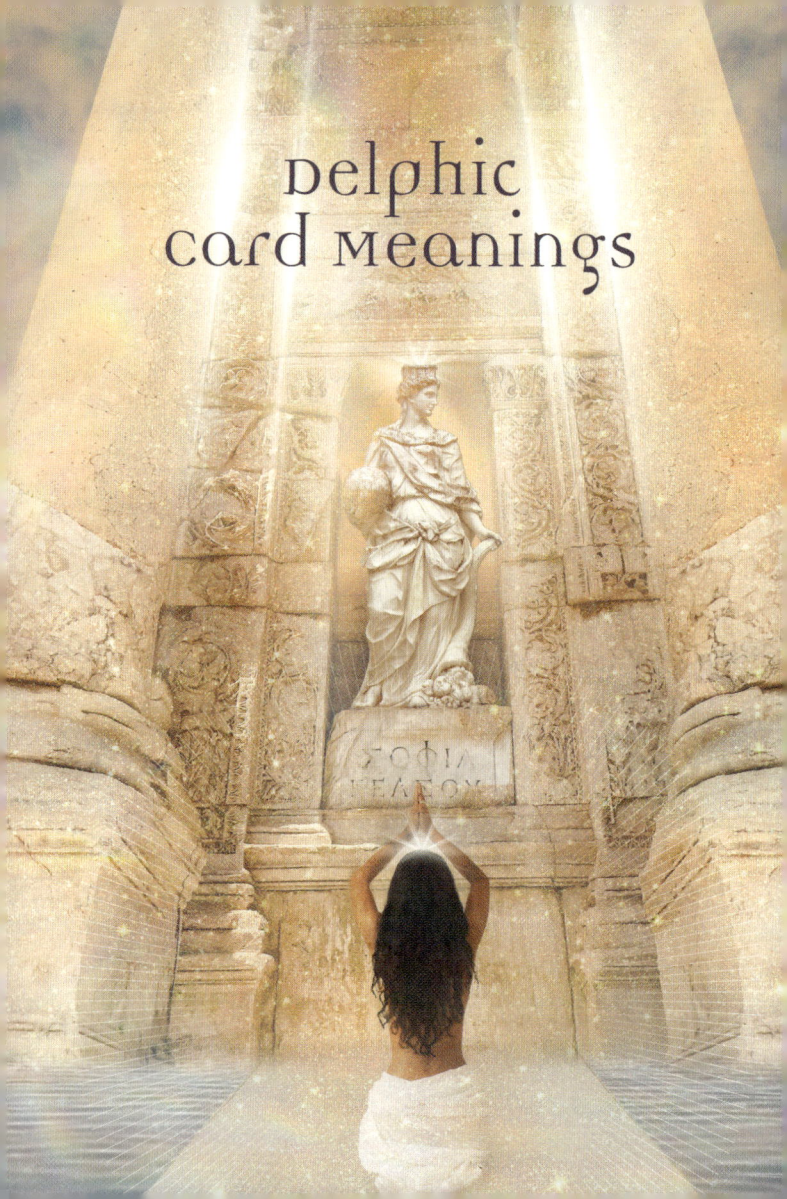

1. PRIESTESS
Begin · Perceive · Predict · Prophesise

Today is a new day and a fresh cycle begins!
As the tides flow and the crescent moon glows,
the Priestess ignites sparks of creative insight!

In euphoric trance, the High Priestess of Apollo channels universal wisdom to open you to the Divine. On either side of her stand two golden pillars, marking the portal to her mystical temple, the Temple of Apollo.

The red wisdom-keeper entreats you to follow your sacred leadership path and wholly embrace your intuitive gifts. You are being called to step onto your priestess pathway with a sense of unwavering devotion, to lead with whole-hearted dedication to uplifting universal consciousness.

The pilgrimage of the red veil is the journey of reclaiming your priestess lineage to restore your divine feminine power. The veil represents life force energy, and the seen and unseen mysteries. Unlocking your ancient wisdom and soul memory accelerates your growth.

Embarking on this journey of self-discovery requires commitment and devotion. You are asked to reconcile and release wounds and limiting beliefs so that you can embody your authentic essence, activate your divine blueprint and awaken the world.

Your connection to Source is endless and ever-unfolding. Being human and spiritual, you have the natural ability to unite heaven and earth. Your own healing journey is a natural consequence of embracing your purpose. We are all connected — by helping others, you heal yourself.

Your cyclic nature, authentic essence and higher calling support your priestess mission. There is strength in your gentleness, so embrace your softness, dear heart! Your actions will have the most impact when you lead with compassion, love and a profound sense of spiritual service.

Read between the lines to see a higher perspective. Remember, the things that broke your heart also opened your eyes. Feel your emotions without judgement to transmute past pain into peace.

Most of the darkness in your life is because you are blocking your own light by undervaluing your brilliance. Step forward and embrace your crown of spiritual service.

Honour your body, tap into the ancient mysteries and become a clear and poised channel for Spirit. You've got this!

The Oracle's Prophecy:
A leadership opportunity is opening for you.

Chakra:
Crown — Higher consciousness and devotional service.

Talisman:
The Priestess wears a red robe denoting feminine life force. She holds a laurel sprig that signifies Apollo's love for humanity.

Faith in Action Step:
Foretell the future. Scry (look deeply) into a crystal ball or other reflective object or surface to visualise significant insights.

Alignment Activation:
Honour your sacredness and announce with conviction:

I trust my connection to the Divine. Intuitive messages flow freely to me. I have clear psychic visions that guide my higher mission.

Artist Insights:
- Priestess path
- Awakening intuitive gifts
- Divine feminine codes.

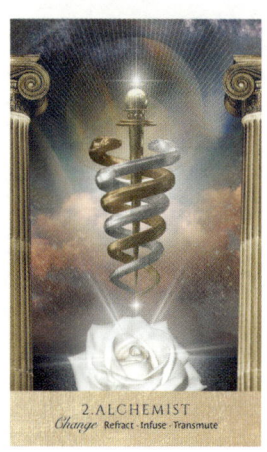

2. ALCHEMIST
Change Refract · Infuse · Transmute

In the winds of change, you find your clear direction!
Entwine, bend and ascend to reclaim and unfurl your
golden wings of light.

Apollo gifts you the magical staff of healing, truth and prophecy to ignite your inborn medicine. This key unlocks the doorway of your transformation and renewal. The serpents ascending the healing rod symbolise a rebirth arising for you. The white rose is imbued with the sweet-scented fragrance of hope.

Spiritual alchemy guides you to listen to your soul — your purest source of wisdom, creativity and inspiration. This voice reveals your divine purpose for this lifetime, and supports you to overcome obstacles, accelerating your spiritual growth and healing.

Know that you are never broken — you might just feel a temporary fracture of the mind, body and soul connection at present. Your body temple is crying out for balance, love and nourishment on all levels. Pay attention to the intuitive whispers, as everything you need is already within your sacred shrine.

You are an alchemist who has the spiritual aptitude to illuminate the shadow and transmute pain into power. When darkness is kissed by the light, it is transformed into hope. Open your heart to receive celestial rays, embrace the uncertainty and enjoy the journey of becoming. Soar into the sun-drenched light of a new dawn! Be the radiant essence of optimism!

The Alchemist archetype is the ultimate problem solver, gamechanger and soul innovator! Transform unhealthy habits through an overhaul of your daily routine and rituals. It's time to turn things around!

Surrender to the alchemic cycle of decay and rebirth. When you harness your bravery to release and relinquish the old, you make way for the new.

Conscious transformation comes from deciding what you truly want and going after it. Initiating positive change and a new direction takes determination. Converting challenges and obstacles into opportunities to learn and grow is an intentional process. Reframing limiting beliefs with optimistic self-talk is alchemy in motion. All change can feel strange at first, so be patient and trust in the process.

Change sprouts new growth. Change summons you forth. Change is inevitable. Embrace it!

The Oracle's Prophecy:
You are experiencing an alchemical cycle of rebirth.

Chakra:
All seven main chakras, aligned along the spine.

Talisman:
The white rose symbolises transformation, purity and peace. The snake staff signifies alchemy and healing.

Faith in Action Step:
Make a list of what you can let go of to make space for the new possibilities that are emerging.

Alignment Activation:
Recite with meaning:

I welcome the alchemy between spirit and substance. I change the frequency of my thoughts and infuse them with the essence of love to consciously create miracles in my life.

Artist Insights:
- Freedom from past pain
- Transmuting darkness into light
- Victimhood to victory!

3. ARCHER
Focus · Align · Pivot · Surrender

Belief drives action! With unwavering faith and forward motion, aim, shoot and hit the target. Momentum sustains success!

The Archer shoots her bullseye through groundwork, precision and full awareness. Implement these strengths to hit your target! Get clear on your core values and set aims that align with them. Eliminate the 'good enough' goals that are getting in your way.

Keep your eye on the prize! Your intention, focus and vibrational alignment will help you hit your mark. Be tenacious about your dreams and adaptable in your methods. Flexibility creates magic in motion.

Know that obstacles are just detours in the right direction, so when something challenges you, declare to the Universe, "I strategise, twist and move on!" Release what you cannot control, concentrate on what is working and trust in a higher power. This pivotal shift will convert a breakdown into a breakthrough for you.

Abandon unnecessary worry that may be holding you back from reaching your desired outcome. Once you decide to let go of fear, it's off your shoulders and in the hands of the cosmic Archer. Then you can focus on creating a clear and positive headspace to attain your dreams. Trust — in yourself and in the generosity of the Universe.

Overreacting, forcing and pushing only restricts your natural flow. Pursue your dreams with joy, then love and abundance simply become side effects. To take grounded action, anchor yourself in the present moment and the blessed earth. Ask for a clear sign to guide you onward and upward to your destination.

The hunt for more meaning in your life will guide you home to your soul. Remember why you came here! What you are looking for has been within you all along. Everything you need is encoded in your celestial blueprint.

Your booming inner calling to serve ignites your every move. Bring out your hidden talents, passions and higher purpose to brighten the planet and humanity with your unique vibrancy and colour. You have a vast creative capacity and intuitive abilities to make your mark on the world. Focus on higher service and the Universe will match your contribution and support your goals.

The Oracle's Prophecy:
Your action plan is working. Don't give up!

Chakra:
Solar plexus — Personal power.

Talisman:
The bow and arrow symbolise the guiding enigmatic force behind your life and actions.

Faith in Action Step:
Clarify your goals, create a wish list or vision board and make a plan. Hold yourself accountable and celebrate your progress.

Alignment Activation:
Steady, aim and fire:

I harness my full potential. I focus and act with clear intention. I align with my dreams.

Artist Insights:
- Vibrational alignment
- Inspired action
- Make your dreams a reality.

4. DANCER
Shift Dance · Enrapture · Embody

Dance is a tantalising conversation between body and soul. Energetic sensations reverberate through your body to liberate your spirit!

The Dancer moves to the rhythm of her own drum, her sacredness personified. She twirls in hypnotic trance and ecstatic flow, celebrating her connection with the Divine.

Shimmy and shimmer your very own devotional temple dance.

A heartening move in the right direction is on the cards for you! Promising opportunities create a refreshing change and lead you one step closer to accomplishing your wildest dreams. Move forward with absolute confidence, knowing that when you embrace your authenticity, never-ending possibilities open up for you.

Give life to your soul's song through fluid movement, sweeping body language and unique expression. Move your body and dance for pleasure. Feel the vibration of life force move through you. Dance to feel the power of Spirit! Take the path of least resistance to flow through life with ease and grace.

If you are seeking answers about a romantic relationship, keep on dancing to your own tune and trust in divine timing. An enchanted meeting will simply happen by chance. When this person dances into your life, embrace them with open arms.

Embody the loving qualities that you want to call in to your life. Work through any core beliefs that are limiting your capacity to embody love. Be brave. Be vulnerable. Soften and open yourself up to give, receive and be love. Your uninhibited sensual expression will draw love to you.

Step out of your comfort zone, be a little daring and move in circles that open you up to new connections. Embrace your adventurous spirit to explore soulful activities that delight your senses. Seek out friendships and community that raise your spirit, energise you and resonate through your whole being. Love and intimacy flow effortlessly to you when you move in the direction of your dreams.

The Oracle's Prophecy:
Your captivating dance entices conscious connections to you.

Chakra:
Sacral — Creative flow, joy and sensual freedom.

Talisman:
The orange rose signifies sizzling pleasure and passion. This bright bloom immediately raises your vibration to sparkle and zing!

Faith in Action Step:
Get moving! Enrol in a dance class or something flowy and fun that ignites your interest and sets your spirit free. Then show up, shine and move to your own rhythm.

Alignment Activation:
Move instinctively to music that calls to your soul and express:

I dance to flow, calibrate and merge with my internal rhythms and higher self. I surrender to the synergy of cosmic union.

Artist Insights:
- Let go, find your flow
- Dance to elevate, activate and regulate your energy
- Invoke your highest self through the medicine of movement.

5. ORACLE
Lead Ask · Listen · Trust

*The secret to an enriching life is to know thyself.
Self-discovery is a perpetual yet gratifying journey.*

The Oracle leads with absolute faith in the consciousness that emanates from Source. She channels Spirit in reflective trance. Where there is darkness, she shines her loving light to illuminate your soul. The voice of the Oracle is separated from you by only the thinnest of veils — draw the ethereal curtain and connect to the spiritual realm to intuit her wisdom.

The Oracle will guide you back to your path of sovereign power!

Every step of the way, self-knowledge supports you on your journey. Clarify your priorities and values so that you can align your choices to match your truth. Be discerning! Know the difference between your voice of doubt and your intuition. The answers lie within.

Explore artistic expression to discover your innate, intuitive gifts. Know that spiritual signs and messages can be quite abstract. Observe the visions and insights that come through. These offer hints and clues to the deeper, more meaningful messages. Dig deep to find the relevance and significance for you.

Dedicated service to your own personal evolution awakens and strengthens your inner oracle. You are forever remembering, learning and growing. Your ancestral legacy combined with the lessons learnt in this current lifetime make you truly unstoppable. Do not doubt or underestimate your instincts. Trust your inner compass to lead the way.

Be aware of pointless distractions and procrastination as they numb your enthusiasm and postpone your joy. You cannot wait until life is not challenging anymore before you follow your heart and make your mark. Waiting for the perfect time will only delay your happiness. Feel the fear, release the excuses and take the actions that enliven your spirit!

As a natural intuitive, others may seek your spiritual counsel. Lead with your light of wisdom and others will follow you. You're amazingly resourceful, with a deep well of insight and knowledge to share.

Now is your time to integrate the valuable experience you've gained and put what you know into action — in your own life and in your offerings to the world.

The Oracle's Prophecy:
Dedication to your personal growth fast-tracks leadership opportunities.

Chakra:
Crown — Clear psychic knowing.

Talisman:
Lemurian light crystals create a link with the divine feminine, representing unification of the soul, access to knowledge and the wisdom of ancient temples.

Faith in Action Step:
Channel messages from Spirit and share your Delphic guidance with others. Focus on service, especially if feeling jittery.

Alignment Activation:
Breathe deeply and centre yourself. Consciously connect to your higher self and the Divine to affirm:

I trust myself. I know myself. Most of all, I love myself.

Artists Insights:
- Clear channel
- Listening and trusting your inner guidance
- Conscious and deliberate attunement to higher realms.

6. MEDIUM
Culminate Consult · Connect · Convey

Take a breath and listen to the spirited whispers on the wind. Dance with the waves, ride the tide and surrender to the ebb and flow. Set your soul free!

A challenging journey is coming to an end and your long-awaited closure is near.

Honour your heavy heart and relinquish embedded grief by allowing tears of sorrow to flow. Grief is itself a medicine — your tears lighten the darkness of despair and represent loving memories. Heartache is often the price we pay for love. Be patient with yourself — healing takes time. Grief may feel like it never really ends but it does change. It's a pilgrimage, not a place to stay.

After an arduous trek and steep climb up the mountain, you can finally see the summit. This final stage is something that you have been building up to for quite some time. Closure brings a sigh of relief and a sense of pride at how far you've come. It's time to celebrate!

This card also signifies that you have the gift of mediumship. Your ancestral guides and loved ones in Spirit are reaching out — sense their all-enveloping love and comforting presence.

Without the physical anchor of a body, spirits are omnipresent. Their essence exists everywhere at the same time. They are all-knowing and aware of the past, present and future, since time is a dimensional paradigm. Trust their guidance when they appear to you.

Spirits connect in mysterious ways. It will not be a ghost-in-a-white-sheet scenario. Communication occurs through inner dialogue, channelled intuitive thoughts, feelings, visual clues and cognisant knowing.

Seek the validating signs and etheric synchronicities all around you. Trust in the seemingly random, abstract messages. Establish a link with your spirit guides and interact in a telepathic conversation by asking questions, actively listening and intuitively interpreting their mystical transmissions.

Mediumship has the potential to soothe grief and restore faith in the eternal spirit. It helps to transcend feelings of isolation, sorrow or constant fear of change. It is healing for the heart to build a rainbow bridge between worlds to channel messages of hope, healing and love.

The Oracle's Prophecy:
Loving spirit guides are supporting you.

Chakra:
Soul star (located above your crown) — Connection to higher consciousness.

Talisman:
Crystal light orbs signify prophecy and spirit communication. Orbs are transparent spheres or globes of light energy connected to spirits.

Faith in Action Step:
Consider a situation in your life you'd like guidance on. Consciously ask your spirit guides for help and take note of what pops into your head. Journal the answers you receive.

Alignment Activation:
Connect with Spirit and declare with real meaning:

As a medium, I am the bridge between worlds. I am grounded on Earth and attuned to Spirit.

Artist Insights:
- Walking between worlds
- Harnessing your spiritual power
- Opening up your psychic senses.

7. POET
Inscribe Envision · Write · Recite

*Poetry is the divine language of the soul,
the pulse of Spirit in words.*

Apollo, the interstellar poet, is a spellbound magic maker of melodic verses. He announces, *"Mean what you say and speak mindfully, as words are enchanting spells that conjure magic!"*

You are entering a powerful phase of creation, shaping your own truth and forming the narrative of your story. When you dare to imagine your dreams, the Universe will echo it back to you.

You have infinite potential to imagine and invent the life you wish. Your mind's inspiration is a direct expression of the creative force of the Universe, which means your thoughts hold incredible power.

Thoughtforms start ripples that can trigger greater ramifications. In other words, the Universe mirrors your wishes, so be mindful of your internal dialogue and what you ask for.

Like poetry, words expressed with real feeling and intention have the power to invoke the senses and create magic. Emotion fuels the meaning of words — without it, your exchange of ideas may be lifeless. Both the written and spoken word are like poetic spells. They have the power to inspire positive change, and unfortunately sometimes the opposite. So, think before you speak and be mindful of what you write into reality.

Be flexible, adapt and follow your own intuition. If ever you feel a little out of step, intuitively listen and skip to the beat of your heart to find your ideal flow once more. Create your own rules — and break them if necessary. Synchronise your natural rhythm to the earth cycles, as this is where wondrous miracles happen. If you are a morning person, make the most of this time of day. On the flipside, if you're a night owl your magic hour and most productive time may be after dark.

You may feel tested the most when you're close to a new chapter, so remain positive throughout challenging times and be aware of your thoughts, feelings and words.

Regardless of the situation, deep down you know what to do and you always have the gift of free will to choose your own direction. Listen to the poetry of your soul to express authentically and seek a more graceful way forward.

When you trust in your ability to collaborate with the cosmos, you rise to challenges with the optimism and answers to create a harmonious life.

The Oracle's Prophecy:
Poetic and meaningful words are influencing change.

Chakra:
Throat — Creative and authentic communication.

Talisman:
Sodalite crystal encourages creativity and true expression. It supports lucid thought and intuition, along with verbalisation of feelings.

Faith in Action Step:
Explore intuitive writing. Write two pages of unedited stream-of-consciousness each day for a week and see what insights emerge.

Alignment Activation:
Trust in the process and declare:

My words have creative power! I have an inborn sense of rhythm — I breathe and sleep in unison with the synchronised tempo of life itself. I trust that the stars align at the most divine time for me!

Artist Insights:
- Self-expression
- Channelling creative outlets
- Turning a new leaf.

8. MUSICIAN
Shine Play · Invoke · Express

Music is the sacred sound of the soul.
Sing your soulful song and synchronise
to the hum of the universal heartbeat.

Apollo, the Greek God of Music, smiles at you! As bright and powerful as the sun itself, he brings the promise of a new day dawning. Every spectacular sunrise provides a fresh start full of golden dreams.

Positivity breeds positivity! Align with Apollo's sunny outlook to experience the divine power of heaven on Earth and embrace the concerto of joy that is awaiting you.

Be your own headline act! Step into the limelight and share your creative offerings with an audience that appreciates and celebrates you for your artistic expression. Have the courage to be witnessed by others to build your self-confidence. Trust that they want to hear what you have to say and will be moved by your imaginings. But most of all, enjoy your moment in the spotlight and smile from the inside out!

Listen to music with meaningful lyrics to inspire and awaken your soul. Stirring music can evoke and amplify your passion for life. Sound has the power to transmute unwanted energies, restore and uplift your spirit. High-vibrational music is, at its essence, the sound of Spirit. Sacred sound baths and chanting support you to remember your own divinity while also healing and balancing your chakras, activating light codes and connecting you to your higher self.

Release any distractions, comparisons or competition. Address any power leakages or draining situations. All of these are depleting your energy and taking you further away from your happiness. It's your choice. Choose your joy and rise with the Sun God!

Apollo also helps you appreciate the unique and harmonious song of each human being. Everyone has a unique part to play in the cosmic symphony, so focus on your own special contribution.

Apollo sings for you: *"You matter! You hear me? You matter and you are loved! Remember the magic of your life!"*

Expressing your uniqueness is your soul singing in harmony with the Creator, so be yourself. You are a precious gift to the planet!

The Oracle's Prophecy:
It's a new day — embrace the radiant opportunities coming to you.

Chakra:
Throat — Harmonic communication.

Talisman:
Lapis Lazuli activates your soul's song. This deep blue crystal encourages honesty of the spirit, opens your psychic abilities and empowers your senses.

Faith in Action Step:
Compose, write or create your own work of art. Put together elements that are meaningful and beautiful to you.

Alignment Activation:
Sing with soul. Affirm:

Apollo, you are my sun! Singing your song enlightens my spirit. This sunlit transmission attunes me to my soul's voice and highest wisdom.

Artist Insights:
- Stepping into the spotlight
- Taking centre stage
- Shining your unique light.

9. ARTIST
Dream Design · Craft · Create

Design your own reality. Step into a state of creative flow. It's time to start living the life you imagine!

You are a visionary — the creator of your own magnificent masterpiece of life! You foresee your dream rolling out before you. Getting crystal clear on your vision and intention brings abundance and boosts your manifesting powers. Designing a dreamy life activates your imaginative, intuitive and spirited essence. Come alive with creative purpose by embodying your artistry and living your dream life with contagious enthusiasm.

Call on Apollo, the torch bearer, and his penetrating gaze will highlight your artistic desires and visions. Showing gratitude for the beauty all around you will bring even more creative breakthroughs.

As the Greek God of the Arts, Apollo is guiding you to see and enjoy the sights of your creative journey. Playful curiosity will help you unearth your passions. Art and creativity come in many different forms. Painting or shaping an Apollo sculpture may not be where your gifts lie. Go within to reveal your creative desires.

Take note, you cannot fool the Universe! Your wistful imaginings must be meaningful to you. Consider investigating a variety of channels to stir your creative juices and awaken the artistic genius within.

Let your inner child come out and play creatively, just for fun. Forget perfection, or whether you think you can or can't draw, dance, paint whatever creative activity excites you. Just enjoy the process — art is the imagination at play. It's time to harness your authentic expression!

Now is the time to bask in your radiance! Like the bright sun of Apollo, rise up, feel the sun's rays on your face and smile serenely. His brilliant sun will be your constant reminder that everything you have ever imagined is within your reach. Open yourself to the beauty in life by actively seeking it. Look around with fresh eyes and let the light permeate your soul as you sense the joy it brings.

It's time to say 'yes' to life again and dream extravagantly.

The Oracle's Prophecy:
Creativity and authentic self-expression spark your inner joy!

Chakra:
Third eye — Creative imagination and visualisation.

Talisman:
The blue morpho butterfly helps you to seek more meaning and beauty in your life. This winged spirit totem also denotes honour and nobility.

Faith in Action Step:
Consciously create a life worth living. Make a list of elements that you wish to include in your best life (e.g., fitness, quality friendships, time with family etc.) What one small action can you take today to move in the direction of your dream life?

Alignment Activation:
Breathe and centre yourself. Affirm with meaning:

I awaken to my own artistic power! I create my inner and outer world with deliberate intention.

Artists Insights:
- Dream your world into being
- Invoke the creator within
- Create a life you love.

10. GUARDIAN
Preserve Protect · Defend · Shelter

Dear soul, know that you are never alone. You are treasured, loved and supported at all times. Take comfort in knowing the light-bearers are watching over you!

A message of reassurance and hope has arrived for you! Your guardians implore you to take the leap of faith, knowing that you are protected and supported.

The temple guardians are caring for your sacred grove, home and loved ones. Their illuminating presence brightens up any dark corners of your life. Tune into their unfathomable love for you, as love heals fear.

Ask yourself: are your doubts and fears merely speculative?

When facing your fears, trust your inner wisdom and consult your spirit guides. Listen to your heart, not your head. Repetitive worry can distort the truth and paralyse you, while deep self-trust uplifts you to wondrous heights.

The well-meaning ego—your inner voice of fear and self-doubt—is designed to keep you safe, but consequently also small and insignificant. While growing pains may not be fun, they can also be a positive sign that you are currently experiencing a spiritual revolution!

Preserve your energy by setting strong parameters and protecting the limits of your personal space. Establishing clear boundaries is an act of self-love. Without them, you give others permission to treat you in a limitless way. Once established, you'll be free to show up authentically, completely comfortable that others are fully aware of who you are and what you stand for. Self-guardianship and sovereign power create a sense of safety, security and steadiness within your whole being. Conserve your strength and establish healthy detachment from unnecessary drama that drains your energy. Create a stable foundation to navigate the best way forward.

You may also be feeling called to awaken the rebel within and break any self-imposed restraints. You are a rebel with a cause! Fiercely protective of your ideals and values, you are a formidable force of nature. Heed the call to step up as a protector of human rights, environmental issues and similar holy quests, for you are a champion of love.

Your courageous action toward positive change is escalating in leaps and bounds! Know that you are making a difference in your own independent way.

The Oracle's Prophecy:
It's safe to step forward.

Chakra:
Root — Balance, stability and safety.

Talisman:
Black tourmaline crystal offers a cloak of protection, eliminates toxic energies and repels unwelcome interactions.

Faith in Action Step:
Consider a situation in your life where you're feeling challenged. Accept the challenge and move forward confidently — do not let fear hold you back.

Alignment Activation:
Steadfast, affirm with conviction:

Love safeguards me with a shield of transmutation. I am a bearer of love, casting out any indifference. I am safe, supported and rooted in the present moment.

Artist Insights:
- Accept the challenge
- Move forward without fear
- Rite of passage and lesson of spiritual strength.

11. SPIRIT
Renew Detox · Purify · Cleanse

Come bathe in these sacred waters! Submerge in this sanctified spring of liquid light to release any debris from the past. Arise, feeling refreshed!

Gracefully floating along the luminescent water, you become fully aware of your own multi-faceted beauty. Spirit resides in everything, including you!

Awaken your senses to harmonise with living light energy. Open your eyes to your sacredness and inner light, regardless of any perceived imperfections. Reclaim your inherent gifts and your natural beauty will be revealed for all to appreciate. This awareness of your own inner beauty and light creates a new sense of confidence that makes you magnetic to your desires.

Strengthen your connection with Spirit! Listen to the wisdom of your higher self. Become a clear conduit for Spirit by stepping into the observer. When your perspective is untainted by personal filters or unconscious agendas, you open a direct line to the Divine. When you fully realise your boundless capacity to link to other realms, high vibrational broadcasts will flow freely from Source. Clear, cognisant transmissions from Spirit guide you confidently in the right direction.

It is time to leave muddy puddles behind and seek fresh water. You are entering a prevailing phase of regeneration. Spirit is guiding you to release any resistance and float freely on a sea of fresh potential. Cradled in the nourishing womb of the ocean, you feel a sense of love, grace and gratitude for the lessons and blessings of the past.

Salty tears wash and clear away any pain to make space for blessed beginnings. Release any past hurts, numbing distractions and sabotaging patterns to thrive once more. Surrender liberates your spirit and clarifies your higher purpose and pathway.

You are ready for a fresh start and a cleaner, healthier way of living. The sky is literally the limit! If you can adopt a more positive outlook, you'll soar into the clear light of love and become the change you wish to see.

Nature revives your spirit and excites your soul. It's time to get inspired about the change of seasons, the whir of the ocean, a glorious sunset, the scent of rain and the magic of starry nights.

The Oracle's Prophecy:
Clear as crystal, you know what to do! Arise, afresh!

Chakra:
Crown — Intuitive transmission of pure Source wisdom.

Talisman:
White feathers are a sign that your spirit guides are nearby and giving you soft nudges of reassurance and love.

Faith in Action Step:
Swim in the ocean, pour a luxurious bath, visit a waterfall, lake or similar, to purify your mind, body and soul.

Alignment Activation:
Bathe in the light of love, see through to the other side. Affirm:

I plunge into liquid light of liberation to flick the activation switch. I am a clear conduit for Spirit and my soul light shines bright.

Artist Insights:
- Doorways to the Divine
- Cleanse to connect
- Become a clear conduit of Spirit.

12. TEMPLE
Sanctify Devote · Commune · Reflect

Return to your inner temple. Open your heart, connect to Source and become one with the Divine. Intention is a magical invitation.

Your temple is where you come home to commune with Spirit.

Set up a sacred space in your home that uplifts your vibration and cultivates a deeper connection to yourself and the Divine. A dedicated altar or sacred space acts as a physical anchor for your spiritual practice. Layer the magic by including objects that symbolise love, grace and beauty for you.

Find your power spot, a place that speaks to your soul and connects you to your higher self. This may be a blissful garden or a special place in nature, within your own home or at your office. It can be as simple or as elaborate as you wish — the main thing is that it is meaningful for you. Your power spot is a peaceful shelter, which calls you home to your core to recalibrate and reset. Your very own slice of heaven.

Daily devotional meditation practices clarify your frequency and expand your ability to receive intuitive messages. Grounding with the Earth Mother establishes a connection between heaven and earth while restoring your natural equilibrium. Take your shoes off and stand barefoot on the earth. Get your hands in the garden. Savour the earthy scent and breathe in the fresh air.

Mindfulness practices help you stay rooted to the sacred now. Breathe and allow yourself to be present in the moment. Pay attention to the intuitive signals that pulsate through your body as these physical sensations are often spiritual validation. Trust your gut, as your intuition never lies.

This card also serves as a reminder to look after your physical body. It is the temple and home of your soul while you are here on Earth. Remember, you are an extension of the Divine. Reclaim your crown and open your heart to reconnect with the oneness, wholeness and holiness of all that is.

You may also be guided to hold space for a circle, creating a nurturing haven for the community to come together in devotional communion with Spirit.

The Oracle's Prophecy:
A sacred space brings you home.

Chakra:
All chakras, aligned and balanced.

Talisman:
The temple keys represent priestess authority and function as an attribute of sacred power in the hand of their holder.

Faith in Action Step:
The power of prayer works wonders. Open your heart to the Divine and your prayers will be answered in unexpected ways.

Alignment Activation:
Arms out, declare with focused intention:

I open my heart, mind and soul to receive clear and insightful messages directly from the Divine. I choose to cultivate, channel and embody my divine essence.

Artist Insights:
- Set up sacred space
- Reconnect with the Divine
- Your body is a temple.

13. LOVERS
Unite Desire · Cherish · Caress

The chemistry of love cannot be explained, only felt with the heart. Love wraps its arms around you. Love is pure, unconditional acceptance.

The starry-eyed Apollo and Daphne signify that a flourishing love is coming for you. Sparks are flying! The attraction between you is electrifying.

You are being called to fully embrace each other. Whole-hearted love requires vulnerability and complete surrender.

If you are in a relationship, this may mean a reawakening of your passion or that a further commitment is unfolding for you both. The full moon amplifies your love and your ecstatic rapture even more.

Your sacred union is infused with a profound spiritual connection. True love evolves with deep commitment and care!

This message may also signify that you cannot force a loving connection. It is not about you. If the stars are not aligning with a current love interest, do not take it personally.

Embody the loving qualities you want in your relationships. Self-devotion is a magnet for boundless passion, love and a spiritual union. Clarify how you want to feel in your relationships and only stay where you are valued, heard, seen and respected.

If you are in a toxic relationship, this card serves as a reminder that you deserve a love that is pure, true and unconditional. Love yourself enough to know when it is time to let go of a connection that brings you more sorrow than joy. Invite in balanced, conscious connections that are fully available to you. Get crystal clear about the non-negotiable values you want to share. True love awaits you on the other side!

The blue lotus in this mesmerising art is often referred to as the dream flower. In the ancient Mediterranean, the hallucinogenic essence of its leaves was known to be mind-expanding and the intoxicating fragrance an aphrodisiac. It was believed to tempt a state of intense longing for union with another. The spirit of the blue lotus heartens you to dream your beloved into existence. It all starts with self-love. If you can see love, feel love, know love and be love, then you can fully embrace love.

The Oracle's Prophecy:
Intoxicating love is in the air!

Chakra:
Heart — The vortex of multi-faceted love.

Talisman:
The blue lotus denotes the pursuit and attainment of euphoric love. As a natural aphrodisiac, it is said to connect one to the Divine, induce higher states of love conscious and enhance desire, passion and intimacy.

Faith in Action Step:
Cultivate deep self-love so that you have an abundant overflow of love to share with others. Stand in front of a mirror, look lovingly into your own eyes and state out loud three things you love about yourself.

Alignment Activation:
Lean into your heart and state:

By your grace, I attune to the highest vibration of love. I embody the qualities I want to attract into my love life. Meaningful connections deepen my love quest.

Artist Insights:
- Divine union
- Unity of the sacred feminine and masculine
- Euphoric bliss.

14. SORCERESS
Summon Conjure · Weave · Enchant

You weave silver threads of creativity into the mystical web of the cosmos. Join the dots and seek out the synchronistic connections to conjure magic.

The Sorceress has woven her way into your sphere to affirm you have her magnetic powers to manifest infinite blessings!

This oracle message serves to remind you that you are a compelling force of nature. You do not need to chase your dreams when you can simply attract them. When your intentions are backed up by your energetic frequency, you become a magnet for your soul's desires.

Others are drawn to your alluring qualities. They can sense that you lead from the heart and your intentions are pure. Let this always be the foundation of your manifestations.

Declutter and streamline your life, dust away any old webs to clear your energy and create space for new blessings to enter. Optimistic thoughts, feelings and actions will attract astonishing wonders to you.

Call in your secret desires and the creative energy of the Universe will grant your every wish. Ask and you shall receive your wildest dreams. Trust that what you seek is also seeking you!

You may also feel called to guide others to discover their magical abilities. A long lineage of mystical guides supports you. You may think you are learning new modalities, but often you'll be recalling inherited knowledge. Honouring your ancestral guides deepens your magical roots. Integrate this ancient wisdom into the present day to enrich your devotional practices and strengthen your gifts.

Reawaken your natural instincts, connection to the land, ancestral knowledge and root yourself in the depth of the earth. Remember — you are nature experiencing itself as human for a short while. Utilise natural elements in your manifestation rituals. Every crystal, flower and plant essence are imbued with restorative properties. Create a nature-inspired spell to ignite your magic.

Seek the magic in the seemingly mundane to truly appreciate the deeper meaning of life. May your graceful footsteps kiss the earth with gratitude and magnetise miracles to your doorstep.

The Oracle's Prophecy:
Your wishes are being granted.

Chakra:
Third eye — Manifestation through visualisation.

Talisman:
With its web of life, the spider reminds us that all paths in life are connected. You are on the right track because all paths lead to the Divine.

Faith in Action Step:
Set your intentions and create a small, sacred ritual to consciously manifest positive change. Miracles happen!

Alignment Activation:
Step into your Sorceress archetype and declare with confidence:

My natural magnetism attracts everything I desire! I embrace the wisdom of age and flow with the Divine laws of nature.

Artist Insights:
- Awaken your power
- Tap into your magic
- Don't chase, attract!

15. ADVOCATE
Reconcile Uphold · Adjudicate · Balance

*Every deed sows a seed! Ask yourself,
are you planting roses or weeds? Pure intentions
are kernels of integrity and fair-mindedness.*

Divine justice is being served and a fair-minded resolution is being settled upon. Your unwavering faith in a positive outcome is beginning to pay off.

Themis, the astute Goddess of Justice, holds space for you from her balanced and neutral standpoint. As an unbiased advocate, she encourages you to make wise choices. Step back from the current conflict to see the bigger picture. Keep a level head and listen to the wisdom of your heart before you make your next move and final decision. Your heart knows the right thing to do!

Karma is a neutral principle, as consequences apply to everyone equally. Accordingly, there is a cause or a source for every effect and action. Intent underpins the spiritual law of karma. Every ripple causes a wave! As the personification of divine justice, balance and natural order, Themis counsels you to be more aware of your intentions and actions.

Themis guides you to weigh things up from an egoless perspective. Is winning or being 'right' more important than reaching a peaceful resolution?

There is a time to be steadfast about your objectives, but right now it may be more opportune to be flexible and take the higher road. Negotiation requires a compromise. Finding the middle ground establishes a win-win situation that reinstates the natural equilibrium.

If you have enquired about relationships, this card may hold another meaning for you. As the proverb says, "Love is blind."

Love can create potent pleasure or intense pain in our lives. It is a prevailing force that has the power to put you on top of the world or into the depths of despair. Relationships are our best teachers and the quest for love is a perpetual cycle of life lessons.

When you are in the midst of new love, the cosmos is filled with starlight and moonbeams, and everything your new love does is right. That is what the proverb refers to with the idea that love is blind. You are blinded by love and cannot see any of your lover's flaws. During this phase you are loving from the heart, not the head.

Once the honeymoon is over and the reality of life sets in, the head starts to take over and judgement, unrealistic expectation and conditional love kick in. Goddess Themis leads you back to your heart wisdom. Here you see, feel and know unconditional love once more, as true love is not blind — love sees and transcends all.

The Oracle's Prophecy:
Justice is served. A win-win benefits all!

Chakra:
Heart — Boosts empathic understanding.

Talisman:
Goddess Themis holds a sword in her right hand representing divine justice. Her scales symbolise her balanced and neutral standpoint and her blindfold represents her role as an unbiased advocate.

Faith in Action Step:
Weigh up all the facts from an unbiased perspective. Combine intuition with a pragmatic approach to make your decision.

Alignment Activation:
Balance yourself and breathe deeply. Surrender to the vibration of peace and unity. Affirm:

My balanced perspective aligns with the sacred heart. I attune to the vibration of divine justice.

Artist Insights:
- Weighing things up
- Justice is served
- Put ego aside.

16. NURTURER
Seed Conceive · Nourish · Birth

The cosmos kisses Gaia. As new life springs from fertile soil, flower buds unfurl into bright blooms. Butterflies flutter with anticipation, ripe fruit embellishes the mother tree. A bountiful harvest is yours.

Beloved Gaia, Goddess of the Earth, embraces you with her generous spirit, endless love and plenitude of abundance. The Earth Mother counsels and supports you through ever-evolving life cycles.

A fertile beginning is coming your way, but to fully embrace it you must authentically love, accept and cherish every aspect of yourself. Listen to the wisdom of your body to support yourself in nourishing ways.

Mothering yourself and receiving with love and gratitude cultivates heaven on Earth. In this state of grace, your feeling of contentment overflows to others effortlessly. Denying your own needs does not serve anyone.

Like Gaia, you also have the capacity to create life on Earth. Nurture your soulful creations to fruition, whether this takes the form of a project, idea or a child. Stay grounded to anchor your vision. It all begins with a pollinated seed, a creative concept and inborn wisdom. Cultivating new growth through to full term is a labour of love. Know that your groundwork and determination will bear abundant fruit.

As the personification of the Earth, Gaia is all-knowing and nourishes life without hesitation or obligation. She is the midwife that supports you through your labour of love. Seek her guidance by spending time outdoors, surrounded by the magnificent beauty of the earth. Home in the arms of the sacred mother, you flourish and thrive in unison with her breath, seasons and endless bounty.

You are fully prepared and ripe to birth your soulful offering and precious baby into the world. Nurture your creation with tender loving care and you will see a flourishing yield. There is plenty of space for you and your creations.

The Oracle's Prophecy:
A fertile harvest is springing forth.

Chakra:
Sacral — The natural cycle of fertility and creation.

Talisman:
The monarch butterfly symbolises transformation and rebirth. Its short-lived existence reminds us that life is precious.

Faith in Action Step:
Move out of your comfort zone and be open to trying something new. Say "Yes" to new adventures and experiences.

Alignment Activation:
Get grounded and anchor to the Earth Mother. Affirm:

I nurture myself. I am in harmony with the cycles of life. I open my awareness to the expansion of love. I anchor my attunement into the earth.

Artist Insights:
- Nurture yourself
- It is your time to bloom
- Reap the fruits of your labour.

17. AWAKENER
Fortify Soar · Emerge · Strengthen

Rise above the storm and you will fly freely into the clear blue sky. Focus on the boundless possibilities and innovative solutions, not the problems.

Recent challenges have triggered a profound realisation of your divine essence and never-ending connection to Source. Your spiritual awareness has awakened! When you can step outside of the emotion and become the witness, you will see all this is happening for you, not to you. This is an opportunity to rise above life's trials and tribulations, widen your perspective and build your personal power.

You may be beginning to recognise that disappointing breakdowns are actually colossal breakthroughs in disguise. Challenges have the ability to lift you out of everyday monotony and show you the bigger picture, one in which you are connected to the expansive potential of the Universe. Naturally, this higher perspective allows you to see the creative solutions available to you. Wide awake, everything appears clearer and makes far more sense!

Always remember that your energetic focus crafts your reality. Refrain from dwelling on the worst-case scenario. You have a choice! Choose to overcome the obstacles standing in your way. The best defence against procrastination and indecision is self-awareness. Release outdated beliefs and old ways of doing things to seek a fresh outlook.

Deliberately create physical and energetic space to manifest lightning bolts of creative insight. Pay attention to your inspired ideas and downloads. These electrifying visions will lead you forward as you navigate challenges and work towards your dreams.

As the awakened warrior, you have laser-like focus and great faith in action. Faith is the optimistic light by which a crushed dream shall re-emerge victorious. Take the leap! Know that a bright future awaits. Your newfound confidence brings boundless opportunities.

Awaken your creative and intuitive power to fully harness your problem-solving capabilities. You may wish to write down the good and bad points of a challenging situation to discern the solutions available to you.

The Oracle's Prophecy:
Life's challenges activate deep growth and ascension.

Chakra:
Solar plexus — The awakening point of spiritual power.

Talisman:
The lightning bolt represents a sudden illumination of the mind and elimination of ignorance.

Faith in Action Step:
Stop postponing the inevitable. An insight has catapulted you upward, although it may have seemed downward at first. Let go and fly!

Alignment Activation:
Have faith in the process, breathe and declare:

I am the Source of my own power. I am open-minded. I call back my power. I ascend into the euphoria of oneness.

Artist Insights:
- Rise above it
- Hard times bring blessings in disguise
- The greater the challenge, the higher the awakening.

18. SOVEREIGN
Reclaim Preserve · Govern · Remember

A deep inner calling leads you on your path of self-mastery. Follow this profound yearning to reclaim your spiritual sovereignty.

The Greek Goddess Hera, the prevailing queen of the gods, has power over the skies. She wants you to know that you have this same influence! Ruling your realm from the inside out, you have the power to reclaim your divine throne and sacred crown. You are a sovereign being! Embracing your autonomy is both an act of remembering and embodying your authenticity.

No more people-pleasing! It is time to stop overcompensating to appease others, as this only creates leakages in your power and doesn't help anyone in the long run. Seriously, let go and let

Goddess! Surrender everything that no longer serves your higher self. Self-regulation allows you to witness the world around you without reacting unpredictably. This proactive approach prevents miscommunication and taking things too personally.

Radical self-responsibility is a regal superpower! It is a commanding way to create an extraordinary life with thriving relationships, especially the one you have with yourself. Blaming outside influences only gives your power away, so regain your sovereignty by taking responsibility for your actions and reactions.

Stand strong in your principles, knowing that sometimes the best thing to do is to step back and not engage. Do not waste your breath pointlessly. Sustain your sovereign strength by instinctively picking your timing. Back yourself and don't second guess your intuitive insights. True sacred leadership is walking in your majestic light with independence, honesty and confidence.

Tap into sovereign codes to awaken your inborn strengths. Connect to your soul essence to reign your realm with grace, integrity and wisdom. Remember where you originated from. You are born of the great Goddess and it's time to reclaim your crown and rise, as the sacred leader you were born to be. Step into your light with love and shed all that is unnecessary. Have the courage to be you and live your truth.

The Oracle's Prophecy:
A royal breakthrough is headed your way!

Chakra:
Crown — Connection to your higher self.

Talisman:
The crown represents your self-determining power.

Faith in Action Step:
Daily gentle movement supports both feminine and masculine energies and helps bring them into balance. This might include yoga, walking in nature or swimming. Just 15 minutes a day will rebalance you.

Alignment Activation:
Stand in your power and proclaim:

I unite with my sovereign blueprint and claim my divine essence. I release obsolete masks and remember my magnificence.

Artist Insights:
- Reclaim your power
- Stand in your sovereignty
- Remember who you are.

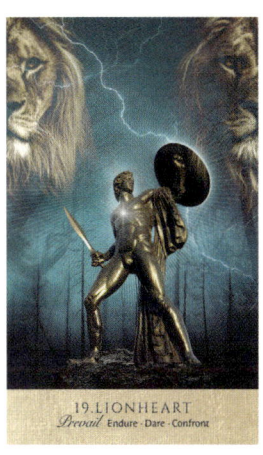

19. LIONHEART
Prevail Endure · Dare · Confront

Brave one, awaken your lionheart! Fall, break and fail — but then rise to heal and overcome. Confront the truth with generosity, courage and diplomacy.

Heracles—half man, half god—bonds heaven and earth. He embodies the awakened masculine qualities of stamina, gallantry, and big-hearted love. He inspires you to do what is right, not necessarily what is easy!

A rite of passage, massive spiritual shift and overall renaissance is on the cards for you. This may involve a momentous transition in your life — a new life cycle, chapter, earth-shattering breakthrough or celebratory win.

Your soul's journey presents immense responsibilities, but you are meeting the challenges front-on with a brave heart. Your determination and resilience prove you have an astonishing ability to recover quickly from tough times and spring back into shape.

Emotional triggers are simply opportunities to learn and grow. Harness your warrior spirit, willpower and patience to overcome obstacles and extract the golden lessons that will make you stronger and far wiser. Wear your battle scars with pride, knowing that these markings symbolise your strength of character.

Courage is the willingness to let your heart lead the way. Heed your heart wisdom and plunge forward with enthusiasm. Take decisive action without overthinking it. Your ongoing victory depends on your ravenous hunger and enjoyment for the hunt. Be bold. Have faith, knowing you were born to win!

Lionheart teaches us that patience, fiery passion and get-up-and-go persistence are superpowers. Continue to face your fears, slay your demons and rumble with valour and confidence. Feats of daring pay off big time!

Walk the path of the brave. Let your soul whisper and your success speak for itself. The real triumph is that you have come home fulfilled, transformed and further evolved.

The Oracle's Prophecy:
After a challenge, you rise stronger and wiser.

Chakra:
Heart — Emotional power.

Talisman:
The lion's shield is an ancient emblem of the sun and symbolises protection and strength, fierceness and bravery.

Faith in Action Step:
Pick your battles wisely. Decide which battles to fight and which to leave for another day, or even walk away from entirely.

Alignment Activation:
Hand on heart, breathe and boldly intend:

The Lionheart activation boosts my courage, spiritual strength and inspired action.

Artist Insights:
- Facing your fears
- Awaken your lionheart
- Divine masculine power.

20. CARETAKER
End · Reunite · Serve · Accompany

In times of darkness, turn to your inner light.
Look up to see the ray of sunlight shining down on you.
The dark winter is reawakening into spring.

You are currently undergoing the natural cycle of death and rebirth. Endings come in many varied forms: a separation, a job finishing up or purely a culmination of a lifecycle. Trust this ending is actually a promising new beginning! You can finally breathe a sigh of relief and blossom once more.

The Greek god Hades and his beloved goddess Persephone represent the cycle of the seasons. Surrender to your natural cycles to honour your light and shadow.

Hades, Greek God of the Underworld, represents the spirit realm, the subconscious and your shadow or ego-self. He supports you to heal through the growing pains of heartache. There is profound growth and transformation throughout the grieving process.

As custodian of the Underworld, his jurisdiction is not an abyss for punishment or retribution, but a regal palace for rest and reawakening, where everyone is returned to the depths of the earth for soul revival. The rivers of Hades' sanctuary run deep. Duality creates contrast. The divine balance of light and shadow, like night and day, is not good or bad, it simply just is. Hades encourages you to honour your perpetual life journey and the inevitable changes it brings.

Goddess Persephone, Queen of the Underworld, personifies the life and death cycle. Forever young, she emerges above the earth each spring, symbolising fertility and immortality. When she returns below ground to reunite with Hades in winter, she is the bringer of death and rebirth.

Persephone wants you to know that you don't need to find the strength to hold on, but instead to surrender and let go! Deep in the caverns of death, you'll find the seeds of life. Relinquish the past to make space for renewal. Trust the blossoming of a fresh start! After the darkness of winter, there is golden sunlight, fresh buds bloom, and the earth comes to life again.

The Oracle's Prophecy:
An ending is a blessed beginning.

Chakra:
Earth star — Located at the soles of your feet. Roots you to Gaia for soul revival.

Talisman:
Hades' two-pronged pitchfork is a symbol of sacred power. His sceptre and ceremonial staff hold the key to his underworld kingdom.

Faith in Action Step:
Start an inner dialogue with your shadow or ego. Avoid shaming your shadow. Reflect on your triggers, as these are opportunities to surrender pain embedded in your unconscious mind. Keep a shadow journal.

Alignment Activation:
Connect deep down into the earth and declare:

I am made up of both light and dark. I go within my inner cave to wholly accept myself! I flow with the river of least resistance to be reborn anew.

Artist Insights:
- Facing and embracing the shadow self
- Finding the light within darkness
- Endings and new beginnings.

21. MESSENGER
Proclaim Guide · Announce · Counsel

In the heights of cosmic oneness, ancient wisdom and infinite streams of higher consciousness flow freely to you.

Spirit messenger, you are a radiant beam of intuitive light and insight! It is your mission to uplift hearts here on Earth at this time. Truth seekers are searching for your wise counsel, so leap into your light of love, spread your wings and fly!

The luminous moon magnifies your clear connection to Spirit. Rise, merge and harmonise with the infinite. Yes, it's your time to shine your intuitive light! Answer the call of your ancestors, loving guides and the gods and goddesses to accept your higher mission here on Earth.

The Oracle of Delphi is whispering directly into your soul — she invites you to fully show up, step up and be all in. Trust that at all times you have endless access to higher consciousness. Have unshakeable faith in your link to the Divine. Get clear on how you wish to serve. Trust your connection to Source and your soul's wisdom. Open your channel wide to embrace, download and share empowering messages for yourself and the collective.

Clear a pathway to the Divine by becoming an open conduit for Spirit. Step out of ego, doubt and fear and into higher service with a loving heart. Focus on spiritual service for the collective and psychic messages will effortlessly flow to you.

When you share from a place of love, your message will always be received by those who resonate with your frequency. Lead from your highest truth and allow the messages to flow through you. Divine synchronicity will attract the ideal recipients to you, those who are ready and waiting to hear your intuitive downloads.

To sustain your clear line to the Divine, be mindful of the energy around you. Ask yourself: does it feel heavy, light or just right? Follow the lighter feeling and the path of least resistance to soar into higher dimensions.

When you get truth bumps, this is your higher self sending signals and instinctive vibrations through your physical body. Spiritual transmissions pulsate, triggering gut feelings. Trust it.

The Oracle of Delphi walks with you through the veils, treading the pathway of your soul, to lead you to your temple of intuitive light. Know that you are never alone — you are surrounded by your spirit guides.

The Oracle's Prophecy:
No more waiting in the wings. It's time to share your brilliance.

Chakra:
Throat — Bridges the higher heart and mind.

Talisman:
Red wildflowers symbolise the Goddess' gifts of intuition and divine connection.

Faith in Action Step:
Find the courage to share your wisdom and inspiration with others.

Alignment Activation:
Shout it from the rooftops:

I am a clear conduit and messenger for Spirit. I anchor love consciousness into the here and now. I share my wisdom with self-assurance. So be it.

Artist Insights:
- Open channel
- Stepping up and leading others
- Speaking your truth and sharing your unique message with the world.

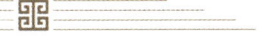

22. DEVOTEE
Dedicate · Inspire · Acquire · Emerge

Your ever-evolving commitment to your sacred quest reawakens your soul memory and expands your intuitive awareness.

Beloved, your higher, most authentic self is revealed in self-honouring practices and rituals. Tending to the sacredness of life aligns you to the vibration of love and restores a sense of balance and calm. Rituals like space clearing, gratitude, blessing your food, meditation or yoga support you during challenging times.

Between the clutter of the mind and heart is a tranquil haven housing your sacred flame of truth. Clarity is attained in stillness and silence. The art of being with Spirit in meditation allows creative light and flickers of golden insight to flood your consciousness.

Prayer unlocks the door to communion with the gods and goddesses. Here your questions are answered, and your creativity is ignited.

Dedicated spiritual habits promote mindfulness. Weave soulful practices into your day. You may wish to write a love note to yourself, reflecting on your own sacredness.

Mindfulness expands your presence and compassionate interaction with all life. It is an extremely personal and potent practice that amplifies your receptivity and capacity for pleasure.

Embodiment gives a human face and physical representation of sacredness here on Earth. Embodiment is about becoming more powerfully present to your holistic experience of life and awakening all your senses to fully accept and express your authenticity. Your body, mind and spirit heal from the inside out when you feel life force pulsate through you. This reverberation heightens all your senses, including your sixth sense.

You are sacred. Walk in your divinity with a strong sense of self. Radiate your light of love.

The Oracle's Prophecy:
Self-devotion supports your soul's mission.

Chakra:
Crown — Devotion to your higher self.

Talisman:
The Goddess is a symbol of spiritual devotion. A dedicated temple or altar anchors intention into the sacred now.

Faith in Action Step:
Press the palms together in a prayer position in front of your heart centre and still your mind. Honour and celebrate this precious moment.

Alignment Activation:
Sense frequencies activating your crown chakra with living light, breathe and say and declare:

I am a personification of the Divine. I dedicate my spiritual service to the highest vibration of love. It is done!

Artists Insights:
- Dedication to Spirit
- Self-leadership
- Inspiring and initiating others.

23. CIRCLE
Collaborate Assemble · Hold · Initiate

Love is an endless circle — complete, whole and absolute. With no beginning or end, the circle symbolises unity and oneness.

Devoted oracles resided in temples all over the ancient world. Together, they adoringly preserved sacred shrines and rites for spiritual guidance, gathering and worship. Seek like-hearted community connections for belonging, support and friendship to strengthen your network.

A dynamic group of well-intentioned equals is circling in and around you at present. Your magnetic vibration has attracted these uplifting connections so you can support each other on your journey. Reach out and engage with this caring community. You don't have to do everything alone! When big-hearted souls join forces, you can move mountains.

Life is not always linear, sometimes you are thrown a curveball and having a supportive network to back you up is both comforting and powerful. Ask for help! Embrace the love of your community. Unconditional reciprocity builds strong ties.

A mutual mission brings you even closer together. By sharing your unique gifts and strengths, your sphere is even richer. Contrasting views, ideas and thinking balances your community with an expanded perspective. Respect the exceptional qualities, values and special contribution of others. Unified, your circle of influence can actually do something significant to make a real difference in the world.

Concentrating on the enormity of an issue that you have no control over can be soul destroying. Instead, focus on what you can do to help. Even small acts of kindness and community service contribute to the overall situation and create peace and unity.

When we come together in friendship, spiritual training and service, we all rise. Even the best of friends disagree sometimes, but when you can resolve issues together, it is empowering for all. Creative solutions are born from collaboration and seeking a united way forward.

The Oracle's Prophecy:
Heart-aligned connections are opening doors.

Chakra:
Soul star (located above the crown) — Stimulates ascension and unity.

Talisman:
The circular ring represents the infinite potential of the Universe. A spiritual quest to the summit signifies oneness, higher vision and many pathways to the Divine.

Faith in Action Step:
Move in high-vibe circles. Seek out aligned friendships and connections.

Alignment Activation:
With your arms open wide, announce to the world:

In higher service, I bond with my dedicated network. United, we work together as one unbroken circle, one powerful force of love and light.

Artist Insights:
- Unity of heaven, Earth and sisterhood
- Sacred gathering
- Collaboration and teamwork.

24. MYSTIC
Know Seek · Contemplate · Philosophise

Discover your 'why' and merge with your magical pathway. Once you know your core values, choices and directions are easily made.

The Mystic attains intuitive insight when in a state of spiritual ecstasy. Expand your state of consciousness to communicate with the Divine or to connect with your own intuition.

Mystic, you are a treasure! Bring forth the wisdom from all who came before you and act as the pivot point for all those yet to come. Your mystical gifts are evolving and this newfound awareness has you asking yourself some life-changing questions.

You may be on the hunt for more meaning in your life. Embrace this yearning — it is an evolutionary shift. As your natural curiosity expands, so does your conscious understanding. With your heightened awareness, you become more sensitive to the interconnectedness and synchronicity between the physical and spiritual world.

Trust in your everlasting connection to universal wisdom. You may be receiving spiritual signs designed to help you on your journey and create a proactive plan. Open your eyes! With faith in the natural order and divine timing, know that everything is unfolding for you with a sacred purpose, even if right now some parts seem unclear.

The Mystic's quest is not so much about becoming anything, but more about unbecoming everything that does not truly resonate deep inside. Steer clear of beliefs and concepts that do not ring true. Trust in your psychic knowing to make sense of life's mysteries.

The synergy of spirit and matter is the Mystic's way. Determine your values and views from both a logical and a psychic perspective. Bringing together the practical and the intuitive creates a balanced outlook.

Step forward confidently on your soul's path with your vision and values in mind. Do not worry so much about the 'right' path to take, as there are many routes to your desired destination.

The Oracle's Prophecy:
Mystic, you are a sacred vessel of divine wisdom.

Chakra:
Crown — State of grace.

Talisman:
The flower of life symbolises creation and how all life comes from one sacred Source.

Faith in Action Step:
Look for and intuitively interpret the spiritual signs and patterns around you. There are no coincidences.

Alignment Activation:
Reflect on the Mystic card. Go within to connect with your inner knowing and affirm:

I am initiated into spiritual mysteries that give my life meaning and purpose. Living with mystery excites my soul.

Artist Insights:
- Trust the signs
- You already know
- The answers are within.

25. SEER
See Enlighten · Visualise · Interpret

Your masks of illusion are vanishing before your very eyes. Clear psychic sight reveals the truth untainted by rigid misconceptions.

Child of the wild, reborn a visionary, outside of labels, your innate nature is fundamentally intuitive. Embrace your raw and untamed expression! Get back to your roots to unveil your second sight. Embrace your free spirit and primal instincts to liberate yourself and see your magical vision spring to life.

This is a message to pay close attention to your inherited abilities for you are the Seer!

As the Seer, you sense the unseen. Dive deep and reflect on the oracle card to seek more significant meaning. Random observations are likely hidden clues, so be on the lookout. Notice what signs pop out to you and intuitively discern the relevant meaning.

Your descendants had intuitive powers to see the future and heal with natural elements. The future unfolds before you in visions and pictorial clues. Reading people, events and situations comes easily to you, especially when you fully embrace your inborn gifts. Unlock your natural psychic senses through regular practice.

Go wild, dance barefoot on the earth, run with the wolves, stomp your feet and shake out stagnant energy. If you have felt the call to work with plant medicine, engage in earth-based practices or go on a retreat. This card is confirmation to trust those inner nudges and callings of the soul as they will support you on your healing path.

Spending time outdoors and calling on the support of elemental spirits will accelerate your awakening journey. The splendour of nature stirs your eternal spirit and awakens your dormant wisdom. Experiences of déjà vu can bring revelations. In these moments, your past, present and future merge and become one. Soul fragments are reclaimed and integrated to wholeness. You feel yourself returning to your roots — a homecoming celebration is happening behind the scenes.

The Oracle's Prophecy:
Freedom is attained by awakening your psychic vision.

Chakra:
Third eye — Psychic sight.

Talisman:
The deer's antlers fall off and grow again, representing regeneration. Antlers also symbolise inborn vision and natural instincts.

Faith in Action Step:
Perceive the reality of the situation with both your physical and psychic sight to discern what may not be immediately obvious.

Alignment Activation:
Visualise and sense an indigo light swirling in and around you. Declare with strong intent:

I surrender limiting filters, constructs and views that blur my intuitive vision and innate truth.

Artists Insights:
- Rewilding
- Clear seeing
- Plant medicine.

26. EMPATH
Feel Relate · Understand · Console

Butterflies are delicate, yet can fly through a storm. Rose petals are fragile, yet bloom and emit an intoxicating fragrance.

Heart seeker, as an empath, you hear and visualise the heartbeats of others! Your immeasurable capacity for compassion floods your heart with the rosy light of love. Heart alchemy can transform pain into peace and heartache into unconditional love.

We are all created equal, yet uniquely beautiful, to learn from each other. Wildflowers are equally as precious as the celebrated rose. Understanding other perspectives enriches the human experience and evolves the soul.

As an instinctive nurturer, you birth, mother and suckle your creative offerings with real heart. Like the lioness, you fiercely protect and sustain your divine creation so they grow healthy and bloom into their full potential.

Discover your own inner mother and nourish yourself throughout the birthing process. Create sacred space for yourself and acknowledge how you feel. Self-mothering is the practice of showing up for yourself and listening to what your intuition is telling you with a loving ear. Integrate heart-opening practices like breathwork and meditation to activate and nurture your sensitive gifts and energy levels.

Being an empath is a spiritual strength, not a weakness. It means you are emotionally intelligent and naturally intuitive. You literally perceive and intuit the feelings and energy of others. Heightened awareness means you are attuned to your psychic senses. This intuitive sensitivity often extends into realms beyond the physical world. Celebrate your empathic ability and develop it to better understand what you are capable of.

Be mindful not to let people walk all over you or take advantage of your kindness. It is important that you always value and respect your boundaries and limitations. Surround yourself with tender-hearted souls that have a rosy outlook and truly appreciate you, while also opening your heart to those who need love and healing. In your devotion to spread love and be love, you are embodying the light that the earth needs to heal.

The Sphinx has a body of a lion, head and breast of a woman and an eagle's wings. Perched atop Delphi, the Sphinx fervently protected the Oracle and initiates of Apollo. The protectress of the temple implores you to stand in your graceful power and shine your heart light.

The Oracle's Prophecy:
Your empathic sensitivity is your intuitive superpower.

Chakra:
Higher heart — Connection to divine love.

Talisman:
The pink rose epitomises unconditional love, compassion and deep affection.

Faith in Action Step:
Attune to the universal heart and the highest vibration of love. Let all your decisions and actions for today come from this place.

Alignment Activation:
Arms open wide like expansive eagle wings, lift your heart to align with the Divine and express:

I attune to the sacred transmission of unconditional love. My aura glows rosy pink!

Artist Insights:
- Keep opening your heart
- Compassion is your greatest gift
- Embody the light of love and understanding.

27. ENCHANTER
Magnetise Open · Reveal · Manifest

Your authenticity is a vibrational match to miracles. Call in magical opportunities with your captivating magnetism and spontaneous spirit.

Miracles are manifesting for you! It all started when you envisioned your dreams coming to life.

Excitement ignites your passionate desire. Unwavering belief stokes your sacred flame. You have the boundless capacity to craft magic and create wonder in your life. Align your actions to your goals. Magic in motion requires absolute trust. See it, feel it and know it!

Accelerate the process by embodying the person who has already manifested all your desires. In other words, act and behave like your dream has already arrived.

Manifest your dreams by creating a wish list or vision board. Ensure the words and images evoke the feeling of already living your vision and immerse yourself in these thrilling sensations.

Allowing is the ultimate expression of belief in magic! Release control, detach from the outcome and surrender expectation. Tune in to the high vibration of desire. Create the frequency of your dream life by lifting your energy to match your vision.

When you consciously raise your vibration on a consistent basis, something magical happens. Your spiritual path lines up in front of you, insights become clear and life starts to fall into place for the highest good of all. Manifestation becomes second nature when you master your energetic frequency. You are ready! Take the quantum leap into the field of infinite possibilities and bring your wildest dreams to life.

Always trust your intuition and ignore limitations of the mind. Honour your shadow, acknowledge your feelings and feel the fear. Give yourself the space to gently unpack it and reframe with compassion, self-belief and optimism. You don't have time to waste thinking about anything that is opposite to what you truly want.

Joy is the ultimate magnet for abundance. Enjoy the unfurling of your dreams. In this elated energy, obstacles may simply fall away or feel less catastrophic. Choose wisely. Positive, congruent energy attracts, while negativity repels. Vibe high, magical one!

The Oracle's Prophecy:
Embrace the endless flow of blessings.

Chakra:
Crown — Vibrational alignment to the Universe.

Talisman:
Ravens denote magical divination, prophecy and magnetism. They also bend time and space to help you call in the perfect moment at the right time.

Faith in Action Step:
Evoke magical blessings with powerful intention, strong belief and consistent momentum.

Alignment Activation:
Harmonise your energetic vibration with uplifting music or anything else that elevates you. Affirm:

My destiny is a matter of choice, not chance. I embody an abundance mind and heartset.

Artist Insights:
- Manifesting desires
- Receiving effortlessly
- Opening gateways and portals.

28. SAGE
Advise Acquire · Invest · Accumulate

You have the Midas touch! Golden opportunities flow effortlessly as you embrace your inner sage. Intention, wise actions and strong belief are the formula to bring about your everlasting pool of opulent abundance.

King Midas and the golden touch teaches that every action has a reaction. Wisdom is born out of learning from experience and brings an easy flow of wealth to you.

If you have been feeling a little lacklustre and not enough lately, shifting out of victimhood and into an abundance mindset will naturally allow you to see and experience the limitless potential in life. The essence of gold can be used to balance your auric field and assist in the transmutation of ego struggles and feelings of uselessness or inferiority. The purity of golden sunlight activates your inner joy and self-confidence.

You are being called to intentionally create the life you want. Sustaining a positive outlook opens up a world of potential and hope. There are more than enough resources, love, wealth and opportunities for everyone.

Remember, abundance comes in many forms. Be mindful of what you wish for, as material wealth alone may not bring you happiness, love and a sense of purpose. Choose your thoughts and beliefs wisely, dear heart!

Discernment unearths significant meaning and a balanced, across-the-board approach to life. Like the Sage, have the wisdom to accept the things you cannot change. Surrender to the flow and relinquish resistance to see the bigger picture.

Sage wisdom is one of your uppermost values. Gaining information and a depth of understanding is exhilarating for you. A wealth of knowledge fills your pot of gold. Your passion for higher education fuels your life mission.

Your natural ability to advise others to better understand the world transmutes confusion and restores balance. With this know-how, you invoke a continuous stream of prosperity and herald a new golden age where wisdom is king. You perceive the boundless capacity in yourself and everyone else. Your quirkiness, inquisitiveness and innovative ideas motivate others to express their individuality and creative potential.

The Oracle's Prophecy:
A golden stream of lushness flows to you.

Chakra:
Crown — The centre of a wealthy and wise mindset.

Talisman:
Gold symbolises the purity of the spiritual aspect of all that is. Gold brings luck to those who wear it.

Faith in Action Step:
Attract prosperity to you with strong belief and a clear vision. Transform doubt into solid gold with conviction.

Alignment Activation:
Feeling gratitude for life's riches, affirm with optimism:

My positive attitude seeks experiences that bring me joy, love and a rewarding purpose. Everything I touch turns to gold.

Artist Insights:
- Money flow
- Financial foundations
- Wise mindset, action and investment.

29. HEALER
Cleanse · Grieve · Grow · Heal

Bathe in these luminous waters under the full moon to reconcile grief and heal your wounds. Surrender your tears to the sacred sea of love.

Evolutionary shifts and continued commitment to your healing path are leading you in the right direction. Listen to your inner guidance system, learn to love yourself with unlimited self-compassion and embrace the life you wish to live.

Transcending your suffering is a personal experience, so listen to the wisdom of your physical temple. Your body's transformational capacity is a natural and instinctive process. You may be guided to rest. By restricting movement, physical pain allows the early stages of healing to take place and prevent more damage.

If you have been through recent suffering, or if old wounds are resurfacing, remember that sidestepping the reality of the situation only delays the inevitable. Accept what has happened with compassion. Honour your feelings and allow yourself to feel them fully so that they may be transmuted by love. Tears are the diamonds of the soul. Cry a river if necessary. Let go and let the Goddess comfort you. Call in your spiritual support team and ask for help.

It is time to surrender, so that you may find the get-up-and-go to start a new chapter. In order to heal, you must also forgive. Be comforted knowing that through every ending is born a beginning.

There are two kinds of pain — one that hurts you and the other that changes you. Giving birth to a baby is an example of positive pain that results in a beautiful blessing. Trauma is often a catalyst for unfathomable learning and conscious change. Although nobody deserves to suffer, colossal breakdowns are often breakthroughs in disguise. Pain can activate your spiritual awakening and accelerate your soul's evolution.

Ascension is a collective mission. Through the magic of osmosis, when you heal yourself, you create a vortex of transformation for the entire Universe. Your healing journey may reawaken your own healing gifts, guiding you to learn, practise and teach energy healing yourself.

Holistic healing considers the whole person—body, mind, spirit and emotions—in the quest for optimal wellbeing. The marriage of spirit and matter means integrating science and spirituality. In other words, alternative healthcare practices can complement mainstream, conventional medicine for great results.

The Oracle's Prophecy:
Honour your temple for healing and transformation.

Chakra:
All seven main chakras aligned for a soothing sense of balance.

Talisman:
Clear quartz supports emotional stability and mental clarity. Like the moon, this crystal is a natural amplifier that magnifies healing.

Faith in Action Step:
Have an aura-cleansing bath ritual during a full moon. Use intuitively selected crystals, salts, essential oils, flowers and sacred herbs to clear your energy field.

Alignment Activation:
Step into your sacred power and surrender:

I let go of past hurts! Renewed, I rise in the cleansing lunar light. Refreshed, I reach up to the purification power of the full moon. So, mote it be!

Artist Insights:
- Heal yourself
- Heal others
- Heal the world.

30. WAYSHOWER
Usher Decide · Discern · Defend

Dark moon and starry sky — you are both the shadow and the light, soft and strong, vulnerable and brave, physical and spiritual, always magical.

Once you make a decision, the Goddess conspires to make it happen for you. Deciding what you truly want and going after it brings immense satisfaction. Don't be surprised how quickly the Universe moves once you have decided that you are worthy of what you want.

You may feel like you're standing at a crossroads, contemplating the right way to go. Tap into your inner compass to sense all the choices available to you. Fruitful decision making depends on a balance between deliberate and instinctive thinking. For strength and guidance, ask Hecate, Goddess of the Crossroads, to illuminate the rewards and pitfalls of each option. Hecate's multidimensional facets show you all the options available to you. Call on her in your darkest hour or whenever you have a difficult decision to make.

Dive into your shadow to see beyond the veil of illusion and seek the truth of the matter. Deep in your bones, you know what turn to take. Don't ignore the red flags or warning signs. Trust your intuition and astuteness to make the right call. Stop overthinking, be decisive and have faith in the goddess to back you up. Stand by your decision with strong conviction, integrity and composure.

It is also okay to not know what you want right now. Decide to be okay with not knowing. Look for ways to stay positive and self-encouraging. Live on your own terms, seek your truth and the right way will present itself at the most perfect time.

Like Hecate, you are a wise wayshower. You bring love wherever you go and shine light wherever it's dark. The skill of being able to lead, inspire and elevate others is a decisive advantage in every way. As your life overflows with magic, everyone around you benefits as you easily refill their cups with your delicious run-off.

Kissing the earth, you walk along with your magical moondust and stride in unity with the goddess to weave magic along the way. Craft, create and dream under Hecate's dark moon of endless possibilities. Cultivate gratitude. Notice and truly appreciate the good things along the way.

THE ORACLES PROPHECY:
Consciously discern the right choice.

CHAKRA:
Third eye — Foresight, inner-wisdom and astuteness.

TALISMAN:
Hecate's torch represents the sacred fire of transmutation. The violet flame enlightens your spiritual journey.

FAITH IN ACTION STEP:
Create your destiny and safeguard your freedom of choice. Journal your core values and align your choices and actions with your deeply held beliefs.

ALIGNMENT ACTIVATION:
Ask Hecate for protection and insight while moving forward. Affirm:

All hail Hecate, beloved goddess, light the crossroads before me, so I can see my true way.

ARTIST INSIGHTS:
- Fork in the road
- Heed warning signs and red flags
- Choose wisely.

31. TEACHER
Learn · Upskill · Educate · Prepare

True leadership is heart-centred action and accomplishment, not status. Humility, clarity and courage are essential elements to lead with real heart.

Your hidden talents are rising to the surface to reveal your spiritual vocation. You are embarking on a quest to discover your innate assets and higher purpose in this lifetime. A calling to do meaningful work and be of service to humanity fuels your global mission.

You are a vessel for the Divine that unites others with their truth. Follow the path of your soul and dare to journey beyond the veil. Walking the bridge between the seen and unseen realms gives you boundless insight and experience to lead others.

You may be called to teach others and share your knowledge of divination and sacred rituals with like-hearted souls. Mainstream training, mentoring or coaching is also a strong possibility for you. Investing in your own learning will support you on this journey. Your effort will pay off in the form of gratifying new directions or career opportunities.

As a natural leader, you do not see yourself as superior to anybody else. Unpretentiously, you are a truth seeker and keeper! See past the surface level to pursue a higher perspective and richer meaning to your experience. You are being called to challenge outmoded ideas and harness more pioneering concepts and ways. It is time to ask questions, shake things up, rattle souls and make your mark on the world.

If you're feeling tested lately, even if it appears completely random, know that you are moments away from graduating a significant life lesson. Earth is like a giant classroom. Welcome the lessons as they are here to serve you. Try not to react to others' behaviour. These experiences are your karmic teachers, seeing if you have mastered peace.

Soul mastery does not happen overnight. If you feel you could have handled things better, know that making mistakes doesn't undo the progress you've made. Look back to see how far you have come, but don't look back in anger. Look back to heal and acknowledge how much you have learnt through the growing pains.

You may be guided to enrol in a course that lights you up! Embrace your ever-evolving journey of the scholar, educator and spirit medium. Step up and shine!

The Oracle's Prophecy:
A spiritual calling evolves your soul.

Chakra:
Crown — Spiritual enlightenment.

Talisman:
The sacred scroll indicates higher learning. Talismanic scrolls contain prayers invoking divine protection.

Faith in Action Step:
Retreat and go within to discover pathways of higher wisdom. Reflect, read, study and research to attain valuable knowledge.

Alignment Activation:
Stand in your leadership light and announce with sovereign power:

I accept my sacred calling. I dedicate my service to universal wisdom and the unending evolution of the soul.

Artist Insights:
- Earth school
- Teaching, guiding and inspiring others
- Discovering your soul's mission.

32. LOVEMAKER
Love Give · Receive · Be

A loving heart is the ultimate form of wisdom.
Expressing, attaining and exemplifying love
brings an unending cycle of ecstatic bliss.

A magnetic, sensual and spiritual attraction is on the cards and things could get very steamy if the feeling is mutual.

The Greek god Eros, also known as Cupid, shoots golden arrows of piercing passion in your direction. Good chemistry means you don't need to force anything, so trust your gut when you meet this special someone.

Love transmutes fear, doubt and the debilitating need to second guess everything. When you love and value yourself, everything else falls into place. Self-love is the master key to true happiness! When you fall in love with yourself first, the cosmos will match this loving frequency and attract even more love to you.

Love is the foundation that reinforces and sustains soul unity, while sensuality is the key to unlocking your pleasure portal. Respecting and treasuring yourself first awakens your authentic sensual expression.

Your sensuality is sacred. Feeling safe to fully open and receive ecstasy is a blessed sacred union and merging with the Divine. Healthy boundaries build trust and allow you to truly immerse in a loving embrace. Intimacy of the physical, spiritual, emotional and cognisant bodies mirrors divine love. Tune in to the sensations of your body to welcome the love overflowing for you.

Primal, uninhibited lovemaking is Spirit moving, vibrating and dancing through bodily form, revitalising your cells, sparking joy, delight and creativity. Surrendering utterly to the experience of sensual pleasure infuses your whole being with the pulse of life force synergy. Self-pleasure brings ecstasy. You don't need a relationship to experience euphoria, it's just a delicious bonus to your eternal love quest.

Once you remember that your true essence is love, everything aligns to this elevated vibration. Do not allow anyone to diminish your divinity. Know that you are always deserving of absolute love that is rooted in profound intimacy on all levels — mind, body and soul.

Spreading love comes naturally to you when you are connected to your bliss! Deep-rooted in love, you are unshakable. Nobody can disturb your inner peace when anchored to the eternal love of the Universe.

The Oracle's Prophecy:
Your search for juicy, passionate love is over.

Chakra:
Sacral — The vibrating vortex of pleasure.

Talisman:
The white serpent symbolises chakra alignment, spiritual ascension and pure bliss. Wear the white snake insignia to be lucky in love.

Faith in Action Step:
Establish a strong foundation in love. Grow strong roots to stabilise your core spiritual strength. Write yourself a love letter.

Alignment Activation:
Hand on your heart, breathe deeply and visualise roots anchoring you to Gaia. Affirm with grounded intention:

I am love. I am loved. I am forever rooted in love. I gift and accept love freely!

Artist Insights:
- Sacred sexuality
- Pleasure portals
- Awakening joy and life force.

33. MAGICMAKER
Captivate Touch · Tantalise · Sense

Harness your mesmerising powers!
Believe in your own inimitable magic!
You are pure vibrational magic in motion!

Enchanted treasures are right around the corner! You dared to dream and craft magic in full faith!

You are your best asset, so bring alive your exceptional gifts and strengths with wild, unrestrained self-assurance and belief. Your alluring quintessence creates miracles. Your magnetism is unleashed by your passion. This is how you attract electrifying opportunities to create your soul's desires.

Becoming abundant in your energetic frequency happens long before attaining prosperity in your bank account. Change your quantum field with a strong belief in yourself and unfathomable desire. Awaken all your senses to summon your wishes into the sacred now. Make your vision bigger than your doubt or fear. Focus on what you love. Invest in yourself, fully show up, jump all-in and manifest magic!

Goddess Circe is the most powerful and strikingly exquisite witch of Greek mythology. As a lover of natural magic, she can captivate the power of nature, brew herbal potions and transform energies with her magical touch. You share Circe's supernatural strengths and healing abilities. Consequently, she guides you to craft your own special magic.

It is time to heal your inherited witch's wounds. It's perfectly safe to reveal your magical powers in this lifetime. You are a sparkly light in the world with extraordinary gifts. Trust in your innate magic and connection to Source. Back yourself! Gracefully release any uncertainty and leap in the direction of your destiny. Worrying about how it will all play out only delays the manifestation process. Move past over-thinking and procrastination. You can overcome any obstacle. One step at a time, you've got this!

Stay in your own lane, focus on your own mystical pathway and do not get distracted with poisonous gossip, comparison and competition. Do not be tempted to seek outside approval. It is not necessary to tell anyone what you're doing until it's done. External influences may dilute your intention and throw you off track.

Trust is the foundation of all phenomenal and close-knit covens and communities. Shield yourself from negative naysayers and surround yourself with genuine and supportive networks instead.

Keep your inner circle small, yet robust and sincere. Come together and celebrate your wins!

The Oracle's Prophecy:
Magic encircles your field. Calculated risks pay off!

Chakra:
Crown — High magic.

Talisman:
A blue circle means an evolved perspective. Wearing or summoning a blue circle strengthens spirit communication and psychic protection.

Faith in Action Step:
Bring alive your natural magnetism with confidence, pride and charisma. Dress up to express your authenticity and unique allure.

Alignment Activation:
Conjure elemental magic by summoning the essence of earth, fire, air, water and spirit. Declare:

My tender touch transforms, manifests and heals. Blessed be, Circe!

Artist Insights:
- You are magic
- Tap into your infinite potential
- Put on your crown.

34. DIVINE
Calibrate Connect · Stabilise · Personify

May you walk in beauty, softly caressing the hallowed ground, remembering your earthly roots and endless connection to the Divine.

Divine timing is synchronising wonders for you right now. Destiny is unlocking secret doors and the stars are aligning.

You are restoring your sense of balance. Take a breath and know that everything is unfolding as it should. Preserve your energy and trust in the natural order and divine plan. Observe recurring patterns, as they are the Universe reshuffling everything to bring your happiest pathway into focus.

Obstacles are often divine intervention, rerouting your soul journey to ensure you reach your destination. See these obstacles as opportunities — they present valuable life lessons. Unexpected detours and growing pains are necessary side effects of evolutionary shifts.

Your soul is created from the purest love of the infinite Universe. Seek to gain a spiritual understanding of who you are and why you are really here. This is your blessed blueprint. When you get to know yourself on a soul level, it is easier to align to your sacred purpose and the gifts you were born to bring into the world. By embracing your personality traits, passions and natural gifts, you are better able to understand yourself, as well as help others to understand you.

By the divine grace of the Universal Mother, find your spiritual centre and connect with your soul. Your divinity is your pure essence, located in that intangible place within your core, unequivocally boundless and always beautiful.

The navel is often referred to as the gateway of Spirit. Imagine passing through your belly button — the blessed threshold which gave you nourishment in your mother's womb. This is your sacral power centre, deep in the core of your soul. Here you are forever connected to higher consciousness. Your spiritual umbilical cord is never broken, you have continual sustenance from the Great Mother. So, dear child of the cosmos, trust your gut instinct, as this is a direct signal from universal wisdom. Insights flow through you and from you. Everything you need to know is inside you.

Trust that you know where you are headed. Follow your inner guidance system — the beacon to your true north and spiritual freedom. Brace yourself as the north wind whistles through the divine archway of your life. Commit to staying steadfast and simply follow the tunnel of bright white love and light.

The Oracle's Prophecy:
Everything is falling into place!

Chakra:
Soul star (above your crown in your auric field, also known as the seat of the soul) — The stargate of spiritual enlightenment and ascension.

Talisman:
The golden grid represents divine feminine flow. The infinite portal and creation spiral signify spiritual growth, birth and soul expansion.

Faith in Action Steps:
Consciously connect with your higher self for ascension and spiritual awakening.

Alignment Activation:
Bring peace and balance to your body. Breathe and centre yourself. Place your palms on your navel, embracing your belly and attuning to the universal womb. Affirm:

I am a powerful creator. I surrender and trust in the divine design. I am the pure essence of love.

Artist Insights:
- Remembrance
- Coming home
- Claiming your divinity.

35. ODYSSEY
Quest Offer · Treasure · Celebrate

*The pilgrimage is life's trek, an intellectual
and spiritual wandering of the soul.
Trust in the journey of your own unfolding.*

This oracle card encourages you to live in the moment, seek beauty in the world around you and enjoy the soulful journey.

To love is far more rewarding than to hate. The presence of love will always cast out hate.

As an explorer, your ever-evolving quest leads you closer to the fulfilment of your spirit's destiny. You are a free spirit at heart. Your inquisitiveness and playful curiosity serve you well on this adventure called life.

Relish the journey, not just the last stop! Slow down, take in the view and see magic in everything. Appreciate the special connections, life experiences and natural wonders of the world around you. Know that you are on the right track when you have no interest in going back or skipping forward. Awakened living is not over there but right here, not tomorrow but today. Breathe into the present moment and fully sense the bliss of just being in the sacred now. Your spirit is alive!

You are about to embark upon a wild ride where you look inward and take inspired action toward your desire. From the universal lens, manifestation is self-growth. If you believe it, you will feel it, and if you sense it, you can create it!

Transitions can be joyful and, from time to time, awfully painful. No grit, no pearl; even the most challenging experiences activate profound alchemy within. Challenges reveal valuable lessons and blessings. The way to self-discovery is from trepidation to self-belief, fear to peace, separation to union.

The Oracle is ascending once again, summoning you to connect to your calling and promise to be of service to Spirit, in your own exceptional way. Share your hidden talents with the world. Shine your beaming light for others to follow.

Your soul's evolution benefits everyone. Ascension is a collective process — we rise as one and nobody gets left behind.

Rejoice in the journey! Give thanks for your spirited adventures! Express joy every day and follow the gracious way of the great Goddess!

Our combined consciousness propels humanity forward.

The Oracle's Prophecy:
Love and wonder enrich your life's quest.

Chakra:
Heart — Aligned connection and life experiences.

Talisman:
The Goddess' staff signifies the path of radiance, an axis connecting the spiritual and physical realms. Picture an ornate torch or rod ablaze with light.

Faith in Action Step:
Find inspiration in mystical beliefs and practices to continue on your spiritual journey and live in your own otherworldly way.

Alignment Activation:
Relish in the present moment and declare:

I gracefully embrace my blessed lifepath! I accept where I am at, and I am excited about where I am going. I seek radiance and beauty along the way.

Artist Insights:
- Adventurer
- Mission
- Hidden treasure.

36. LUMINARY
Activate Brighten · Impact · Determine

You are rising from a dark night of the soul and undergoing a significant awakening! The dawn was born with wings of light to lift you to great heights!

Leading light, know you inspire others with your dedication in your chosen field of expertise. Alternatively, you may be on the path to discover your soulful purpose in this life.

Breakthroughs are coming! A major shift has rekindled a strong sense of personal power for you. Rays of light emanate from your solar plexus, just below the breastbone. Your inner golden sun has ignited. This energetic vortex is responsible for your growing confidence, stability and self-esteem.

Clarify your priorities to make life choices that are congruent with your higher purpose. It's easy to make decisions when you know your core values. Living in contradiction to your beliefs always leads to feeling like an imposter in your own sphere. Walk your talk and embody your ideals to live in greater integrity. In other words, ensure that what you say is what you actually do. Having clear, purposeful intentions ignites a strong sense of self that brings confidence and profound inner peace.

Luminary, you are a brilliant light-giving body, like the sun or moon. Life is a golden chance that you appreciate and undeniably make the most of. Fiercely independent in your thoughts and actions, others seek your unbiased counsel and strong leadership. With fire in your soul to live life on your own terms, you inadvertently light the way for others to follow. You make everything seem magical and naturally encourage those around you by merely expressing your vibrant nature.

Some may fear your light as it makes them squirm, but know this is because they currently feel safer in the shadows. Don't be tempted to extinguish your own light to make them feel more comfortable.

As an ancient soul, you prefer life's more meaningful aspects, rather than the mundane. Don't dim yourself down. Engagement with the world, soul to soul, leaves a legacy of love. Shine bright like a lighthouse! Life is too short to let fear drive you back into the darkness. To greet each moment without preconceived judgement is freedom. In divine timing, all lost souls find their way back to the light of love.

The Oracle's Prophecy:
Your sword of wisdom shines a leading light.

Chakra:
Solar plexus — The golden chakra that exudes personal power.

Talisman:
Pegasus embodies creative force, power and support. The white-winged warrior means divine help is on its way!

Faith in Action Step:
Engage your inner strength to find faith in the power of love and live your highest purpose with full-bodied intention.

Alignment Activation:
Breathe, focus on your solar plexus chakra and with loving intention expand your auric field and light body. Affirm:

I exude golden rays of sacred power! I stand firm in my light and truth!

Artist Insights:
- Inspiring journey
- Dark night of the soul
- Dawn of a new day.

37. DREAMWEAVER
Emergence Wish · Visualise · Conceive

*Life is a rich tapestry of synchronicities
woven together with meaningful connection.
Tie gossamer ribbons of faith to your dreams.*

Take your dreams and sew them into your life. You are entering a lunar cycle of vision creation, pulling a golden thread from the realm of unlimited potential and entwining it with the sacred now.

Balance your fierce determination with quiet confidence to birth your dreams into reality. Perceive, believe and achieve! Rise into the light of your ever-evolving soul. Your full-bodied intention and focus combined with your innate creativity propels you in the direction of your objectives.

At first you may be afraid to dream without restraint, but know that you are a powerhouse of light force energy. You are the Dreamweaver! Your aptitude for manifestation is greater than you can ever comprehend. Do not underestimate your abilities. Time and money are an illusion, so focus on your joy instead and a steady flow of abundance will become a natural consequence.

Set your target high, so that you can reach up and grow into new levels. Expand your mind and feel as if your desire is already fulfilled. When you can handle the magnitude of this new elevation, you will rise to meet it. Progressive discovery is far more rewarding than instant gratification. Self-assurance develops as milestones are reached, so celebrate every step of the way!

The rosy full moon magnetises your wishes and attracts abundant resources to you. Pay attention and observe the mysterious coincidences that occur and usher you closer to your moonlit dreams.

Rise above limiting thoughts to seek the opportunities that will accelerate your desires. When you question your doubts, reframe your negative self-talk and face your fears, you realign to your wildest dreams and stitch positivity back into your life's tapestry.

The Oracle's Prophecy:
Aspirations are being harnessed.

Chakra:
Third eye — Supports envisaging your dreams.

Talisman:
The white tiger exemplifies feminine fierceness, creativity and clairvoyance or psychic sight.

Faith in Action Step:
Dream your desired reality into being. Use the power of creative visualisation and your personal strengths to support your dreams.

Alignment Activation:
Breathe, centre yourself and fully commit to your dreams:

I align to my divine destiny! Enthusiasm, intuitive wisdom and practical strategy ensure my dreams manifest.

Artist Insights:
- Act upon your heart's desires
- Make your dreams a reality
- Dare to dream big!

38. THEATRE
Participate Challenge · Co-create · Contend

Seduce your soul and unlock your creative voice 'til it purrs with heavenly delight! Be the leading light of love in your own stage production.

The Greek god Apollo personifies music, poetry, art, archery, healing, sun and light. He guides you to explore your own unique artistic gifts. Authentic, creative and intuitive expression is your soul singing. Life's a stage, so play your part with real spirit!

A portal is opening in your realm. Throw all your doubts out the window as you are well and truly on your way to prodigious stardom. Expect a big break soon! It's your time to shine!

Creative flow and determination have spurred your desire to grow and prosper. Imagination inspires your soul to sing, your heart to open and your mind to expand. Creativity comes in a wide range of exceptional forms — it's not always the obvious artistic pursuits that come to mind.

Seek out opportunities that excite but also scare you a little. When you challenge yourself, step into the leading role and take centre stage, your confidence will soar, and you will overcome any stage fright. Be daring and uplevel the purpose and passion in your sphere. It is time to go for it!

Focus on your unique role and contribution, and do not be distracted by competitiveness. Stop comparing yourself to others. Shift your focus and realise that your unique input is valuable. Never assign anyone that much power over your sovereignty.

Collaborating with the Universe ensures unending triumph. In other words, what you put in is what you get back, and then some! Your soul's potential and infinite connection to Source energy is vast, not small. When you wholeheartedly engage with life, you'll amaze yourself with the applause! Open up to receive all the blessings, goodness, love, prosperity and light into your life.

When your spirit guides sense you need them, they'll come from far and wide to support you. They are your most loyal and loving fans. Open yourself up to their wisdom. To energetically communicate with your spiritual guidance squad, simply send them a message in your thoughts.

If you're an actor, you could have someone on your spirit team who was once a performer too and now wants to mentor and inspire you as an artist. Their shining example motivates you ever more. Stay on the lookout for signs from your spiritual council. Know the Universe really does have your back!

THE ORACLE'S PROPHECY:
Your consistent effort is being rewarded.

CHAKRA:
Third eye — Centre of imagination.

TALISMAN:
The theatre mask acts as a sign for you to unmask yourself and stop hiding. Masks may also represent leading ancestral and spirit guides.

FAITH IN ACTION STEP:
Life requires your participation, so take part in an activity that grows your knowledge and confidence. Join a choir, course, theatre group or whatever you feel stretches you.

ALIGNMENT ACTIVATION:
Step into the spotlight and affirm:

I'm the leading actor in my own play! I fully show up and come to the front of the stage, take my curtain call and bow to the standing ovation and audience's applause.

ARTIST INSIGHTS:
- The divine play
- Accepting challenges
- Unmasking yourself.

39. SANCTUARY
Relax Soothe · Revive · Return

*Come home to your heart temple.
Self-devotion is an act of love, so go within your
blissful bubble to feel alive and thrive!*

Shelter from the storm, as the turbulence will soon pass. Wait it out and take this opportunity to recalibrate and restore your peace of mind. In between repetitive thought, incessant worry and high emotions dwell your still centre and a comforting silence. Intuitive clarity and a deep pool of inner knowledge resides within your heart.

Spend time in nature to harmonise with the natural rhythms of life. Take time out, rest a while, fill up your precious vessel and be reassured that you are entering a powerful period of transformation and healing. Mindfulness meditation, breathwork and similar devoted practices will help sustain your natural equilibrium and sacred balance.

Return home to your heart to replenish your eternal reserve within! A deep-rooted sense of belonging connects you to euphoric oneness. Balance quality time for yourself with the company of like-hearted souls to recharge.

Take back what is yours, by way of free choice, and decide what you invest your energy into. You may be purposely detaching from toxic drama and evolving past the triggers that once dragged you in.

Be thankful for the life lessons that return to challenge you and your soul's evolution. Devote time to what adds value and enriches your life. Seal the leaks that deplete your precious life force. There are no weak moments, only trials of strength. You have the fortitude and intuitive wisdom to effectively manage your inner and outer worlds with integrity, ease and grace. Lean on your inner strength during this time.

Another more pragmatic meaning for this oracle indicates that you may be undertaking a renovation, rebuild or an upgrade of your home. Be comforted knowing that your planning and preparation will pay off. A happy move may be on the cards for you, so chin up and start packing!

A house is not a home unless it is infused with love, laughter and joy. Creating a blissful, light-filled space nurtures and nourishes your spirit. Open your doors and invite love to fill your heart and home.

Start by creating a special space just for you. Self-care is a beautiful expression of self-love. Practise self-honouring rituals until they become natural and routine for you.

The Oracle's Prophecy:
A well-deserved break revives the spirit.

Chakra:
Heart — Return home to your inborn nature.

Talisman:
The life-affirming gemstone emerald calms the spirit and heals the heart!

Faith in Action Step:
Start each day by imagining an emerald green light infusing your heart and filling your aura with loving energy.

Alignment Activation:
Imagine you are breathing in the fresh scent of a temple garden. Recite with heartful intention:

I am home. I am safe. I belong here. I continually rejuvenate. Thank you for my perpetual healing!

Artist Insights:
- Relax
- Recharge your batteries
- Rest.

40. ILLUSIONIST
Divert Spellbind · Revamp · Unveil

I am the mirror of the One. As the cosmos, so the soul!

See beyond the veil to find the hidden meaning — not everything is as it appears to be right now. Beware of tricks that deceive the eye. 'Smoke and mirrors' may distort the truth. No matter how much you know, there will always be the unknown.

Remove your rose-coloured glasses to see the truth! Open your eyes to see a more expanded viewpoint. Scratch beneath the surface and look past the obvious as there are much more important things at stake right now than what is immediately in front of you.

Tap into your full potential, especially now when you need to unmask the truth. You already have the resources and insight you need to make sense of this mystifying state of affairs. Once you have a clearer picture, head off any imminent danger and reroute to a higher state of awareness.

The Universe is full of mirrors and reflections, including your own mind. Your life experience is made up of how you think about and interpret the world around you. Your interactions with others are reflected back at you. See this is an opportunity to get to know yourself better.

Perhaps it's time to hold the mirror up and bravely do the shadow work that you are being called to. This is where true self-mastery takes place. Remember, you are the light bearer to your own darkness! You have the skills to go within to bring light to any limitations that are holding you back.

Inner work reveals self-sabotaging patterns that are ready to be brought forth and healed. Take the time to be in your body and sense its subtle energies. Ask for inner guidance and learn how to listen to the voice of your soul. Trust your raw instincts and unveil your ability to heal yourself.

Embody your truth and the Universe will mirror your authentic frequency. What are you passionate about? Your passions are your priorities. Align your choices to those priorities and the Universe will reflect that back to you.

As the Illusionist, you are a talented conjurer who performs great feats. Sometimes you want to stand out and other times you want to blend in, occasionally hiding away to recuperate and other times wishing to stand out to make your mark. Similarly, gracefully bowing out of situations that no longer excites you creates space for red-hot desires.

The Oracle's Prophecy:
Hidden messages are being revealed.

Chakra:
Root — Solid foundation for life.

Talisman:
Mirrors represent light and truth, while the mirror amulet also offers a reflective shield.

Faith in Action Step:
Standing in front of a mirror, gaze deep into your eyes and see what is revealed to you. The eyes are mirrors of your soul.

Alignment Activation:
Seek beyond the red flame of misconception and declare:

I am seeing clearly beyond my illusions. I see others as divine reflections of myself. I see beyond the hoax of separation.

Artist Insights:
- Smoke and mirrors
- Deception and trickery
- Moving beyond the illusion of separation.

41. FAITH
Hope Anticipate · Aspire · Foresee

Clear credence sings the song of the heart!
Grace supports boundless self-belief! Surrender, walk
with faith and trust in the power of the Divine.

Listen to the spirit whispers from the other side. You are entering a new phase of life. It is time. Step up with strong belief in your inborn and learned abilities. Be certain of your own capacity to move forward fearlessly. Self-reliance spurs you headfirst into a bright future. Your crystal-clear vision guides you forward onto your golden pathway.

Tap into the utmost influence of faith, hope and love. If you are finding it challenging to embody your self-trust, rely on the higher power of universal love. Faith it until you make it, braveheart!

The Goddess supports your every move! The Universe has you covered! It is safe to follow through with your new plans. When you lead with your heart and self-assurance, everything will fall into place. Be brave and get out of your comfort zone. Take the first step in faith, trusting that the next step will magically appear as you sense your way forward. You are a leader of light! Pioneer, jump forward with faith in action. Do not stay in places you have outgrown!

You may have been let down by people around you in the past. Allow the power of love to heal your heart and reinstate your confidence in life and relationships, so you can glide gracefully forward. Find the golden lessons hidden in the pain of previous disappointments. The past makes you wiser, more discerning and clearer on your values and priorities. This refined clarity makes you more perceptive of people and situations.

Leave the past in the past and stop worrying about the future, as you only ever have the present moment. Divine timing is a powerful force that synchronises opportunities to happen at the right time and for a significant reason. Trust that your life is unfolding in a meaningful way. Try not to control it.

Deep down you know what you want for yourself. Stop fixating on the future and regretting the past. This is your time to soar. You have been waiting for this moment to rise and stride gracefully into the rainbow light to be reborn. Astonishing surprises await you on the other side. Step up now!

The Oracle's Prophecy:
Optimism returns bringing joyful blessings!

Chakra:
Heart — Carries hopefulness.

Talisman:
The golden gateway represents a heart portal of universal love that helps you defeat your inner demons and gain self-belief.

Faith in Action Step:
Gather the courage to leap with unfathomable faith! Do not look back. Move forward with strong belief and an open heart.

Alignment Activation:
Look ahead and step up with hope in your heart. Declare to the Universe:

I flow with faith! I trust the Divine supports my every move. My confidence builds with every step!

Artist Insights:
- Step forward with faith
- Get out of your comfort zone
- Trust that the Universe has your back!

42. SEEKER
Expose Heed · Appraise · Face

You are the treasure hunter — awake, aware and alert to the synchronistic signs. Consciously follow the labyrinth of self-discovery to find the hidden gems along the way.

Pandora warns you to tread carefully and consider the potential consequences of your actions before you make your next move. Once that door is opened, there is no turning back! Ask yourself, "Am I playing with fire?"

Softly does it! Act upon your curiosity in a watchful and considered manner. Use careful judgement to ensure a well-considered response. In other words, think and sense consciously before you speak and act. Every action has a reaction!

Proceed with caution. Open your psychic senses to intuit all possible scenarios before making a thoughtful choice. Be mindful of your real intentions and reasons before you give free rein to your curiosity. Temptation and senseless snooping may generate havoc and trigger a series of unwelcome events.

Everything is interconnected. Like a game of dominoes, once one domino falls, it starts a chain reaction. Unleashing chaos to initiate a reaction for no good reason only creates disharmony. Some things are better left unsaid and untouched. Karma is the natural law of cause and effect. It is impartial and very tangible. Be reassured — the natural order of things will be sorted out by the karmic flow.

Curiosity might have killed the cat, but gratification brought it back! While prying may harm you, the satisfaction of discovering the truth may also be worth the risk. Weigh up the possible outcomes. Even if you don't like what you see at first, you may prefer to know the reality of the situation. Only you can make the call. Look for the signs and trust your intuition. The truth will always set you free!

This card also suggests there may be more than one answer or solution to your predicament. Formulating a forward plan with grace, intuition and thoughtfulness will produce a positive outcome. Measured curiosity fuels your playful and creative nature. As a resourceful and creative thinker, your intense curiosity makes you receptive to innovative ideas. Open your spiritual toolbox to intuit the most productive way onward and upward!

The Oracle's Prophecy:
Undercurrents create consequences.

Chakra:
Solar plexus — Governs personal freedom and choice.

Talisman:
Pandora's box of repercussions is a reminder of the virtues of willpower, thoughtful consideration and patience.

Faith in Action Step:
Uncover the truth. Do your due diligence. Face up to the part you played in a situation and the subsequent results.

Alignment Activation:
Go within to understand your curiosity and to decipher your real intentions. Affirm:

I trust that I will make the right choice moving forward. I understand that my actions create outcomes.

Artist Insights:
- Truth coming to light
- Karmic cycles
- Consequences of actions.

43. SHAPESHIFTER
Ruffle Cease · Bewilder · Shake

Slinking, changing and courageously maneuvering through a dark night of the soul, you arise reborn into a glorious sunrise.

A long-awaited ending prompts a drastic reorganisation that revolutionises your life. Obsolete constructs are crumbling to make space for this restructure. This break with the past overhauls your world and sets in motion a torrent of exhilarating possibilities.

Be reassured, as an intuitive communicator, you have the natural ability to adapt, fit in and be accepted in any new surroundings. This litheness and capacity to camouflage and disguise yourself at will shields you from individuals and groups that no longer resonate with you. Your exit happens so gracefully that no one is perturbed by your swift departure.

It is now your responsibility to ensure there is not a repeat performance. True awakening requires a renewal of the mind, heart and soul. Seek the lessons and appreciate the growth, as it's a complete change for the better!

Shapeshifter, you have the ability to change, adapt and transform at will. Nothing ever stays the same. We are all ever-evolving. Change is inevitable, yet growth is purely optional. Elect to learn and grow through change and upheaval. Trust yourself to consciously create change.

A black panther spirit guides you to understand the deeper meaning of your life's cycles, supporting you through your different seasons and incarnations. When this regal cat shows up for you it is time to remove any archaic masks. As a shapeshifter, you might find yourself feeling lost at times. Living honestly and authentically is essential to your overall sense of self. Invoke the spirit of the panther when you need the tenacity to stand alone. As an awakened warrior, reclaim your divine power and feline prowess and approach your journey without trepidation.

A raven spirit glides into your jungle to signify that magic is at play! Potent shifts are being realised. Your wishes are being granted. The raven will support you to fly into the darkness of your unconscious mind to transmute any inner turmoil that is currently shadowing your soul light. Deep healing is underway for you.

The Oracle's Prophecy:
Courage to end a situation creates peace.

Chakra:
Heart — The centre of emotional alchemy.

Talisman:
The black panther moves at the speed of light, is decisive, adaptable and highly principled. Invoking the spirit of the panther will accelerate positive change.

Faith in Action Step:
Trust your instincts to adjust quickly to your new environment. Think on your feet and you'll bounce back stronger.

Alignment Activation:
Merge into oneness and visualise the ever-changing spiral of life. Declare with real intent:

I adapt to change effortlessly and gracefully. I embrace my evolutionary shifts with ease and flow.

Artist Insights:
- Alchemical transformation
- Transmutation
- Rebirth.

44. STRATEGIST
Counsel Project · Lobby · Advise

Desire for knowledge evolves the soul.
To discover true wisdom, think for yourself!
Inquisitiveness is exquisite curiosity at play.

Socrates, the ancient Greek philosopher who pondered the meaning of life, implores you to be more thoughtful, curious and open-minded.

Embrace your golden halo of wisdom! As a deep thinker, others seek your leadership and intellectual advice. You have a natural gift of making the incredibly complex feel simple, logical and easy to understand. As a strategic visionary, your balanced approach integrates creative insight and profound inner knowing with common-sense tactics to find solutions that benefit everyone.

It is time to see the bigger picture! Stepping up and advocating for a global cause that heals not hurts the planet attracts like-minded supporters. Collaboration is key! A joint undertaking brings together a wide range of skills that advance your cause. Get clear on your priorities and what is truly needed to support your collective mission. Open your mind to creative insights and innovative ideas. You are a part of an evolutionary shift that unites, benefits and lifts the cosmic vibration.

Wonder is the foundation of wisdom, so trust in your own inner knowing to make up your own mind. Be curious. Ask questions. Explore a wide range of facts and concepts before you make a decision. Unyielding stubbornness prevents you from seeing the opportunities and solutions available to you. It's okay to change your mind and see things from a different perspective. Approaching situations as the observer, not the judge, expands your understanding and wisdom. Being open-minded creates an environment to learn, grow and discern with a balanced vantage point.

Be compassionate. Everyone is doing the best they can with the cards they have been dealt. Kind, thoughtful and respectful communication creates better outcomes for all. When faced with confrontation, stand in your power with empathy. The ability to suspend judgement and see things from others' perspectives will serve you well.

The Oracle's Prophecy:
A higher perspective brings understanding.

Chakra:
Crown — Higher perception and contemplation.

Talisman:
The golden halo denotes spiritual wisdom and connection to the divine mind.

Faith in Action Step:
Dig deeper, study all the facts, find the meaning behind important issues.

Alignment Activation:

Open your mind to a higher perspective. Affirm strongly:

I gather all the intel, seek the deeper meaning and ponder on all the facts before I share my findings. My beautiful brain continually learns. I think before I speak.

Artist Insights:
- Make a plan
- Be strategic
- Take aligned action.

About the Author

Suzy Cherub is a devoted priestess, mystic and wayshower.

As an internationally award-winning psychic, Suzy has helped thousands through her natural healing guidance. As a celebrated author, speaker and intuitive coach, she gently guides and empowers others, nurturing their innate wisdom and inspiring a more conscious, authentic and fulfilling way of life.

Suzy is a matriarch, mama and grandmother who wears her wise woman crown with overflowing pride. As a spiritual adventurer, she has travelled the globe to explore ancient sites, temples and natural wonders. She began channelling the concept, meaning and insights for what would become *Oracle of Delphi* after visiting the site of the Temple of Apollo in Greece. Her creative imaginings are dedicated to weaving magic into the mundane. This is her fourth deck, following the bestselling *Star Temple Oracle*, *Faery Temple Oracle* and *Water Temple Oracle* — and there is so much more to come!

"Cherishing the crone and sage season of my life is a beautiful blessing. I answered the call to honour the sacred way of the Priestess many years ago when I experienced 'dark night of the soul' type awakenings and successive rites of passage. Vivid past-life memories, ancient remembrances and a profound inner knowing unearthed divine mysteries channelled from a long lineage of temple priestesses."

"I have always felt a deep soul connection and spiritual congruence with the ancient temples, especially Apollo's Temple of the Sun in Delphi. It's a humbling privilege and an honour to dedicate this soulful offering to the Oracle of Delphi and the long line of ardent priestess keepers that paved the way for modern-day mystics. May the magical mysteries of the Oracle open your intuitive senses, mysticism, wonder and inner wisdom."

"I acknowledge the Ngunnawal people as the traditional owners of the land that I work and live on, and pay my respects to all First Nations people and Elders past, present and emerging."

Hidden mysteries are seeded within your soul,
a sacred spring of *luminous insights,*
windblown imaginings and ancient ways,
floating like blue lotus flowers on a lilac lake.
Come home to your soul temple.
Sail into the mystique.

In goddess grace and wisdom,
SUZY CHERUB

Join the Temple

The Temple of Intuition with Suzy Cherub is a free online space to share, enrich and fine-tune your intuition. It is a thoughtful, collaborative and open-hearted community of sensitive, spiritual souls dedicated to intuitive growth and soul expansion.

To find out more about joining
The Temple of Intuition with Suzy Cherub, visit:

www.suzycherub.com

About the Artist

Briarly Collyns **is a visionary artist, visual alchemist, intuitive and inspirer.**

She channels enchanting visions of other realms, worlds and times through her form of digital artistry: visual alchemy. Each piece is coded with symbology and sacred geometry to create a unique frequency and alchemical medicine.

Her creative process is simple. "I find the sweet spot between my inspiration, intuition and joy, and the art manifests through me almost like magic! It's not work, it's a divine co-creation with the Universe. I am simply the channel (and a bit of a tech witch!)"

Briarly is devoted to amplifying light, beauty, magic and higher vibrations in the world; whether that be through her art, voice, visions or simply being her authentic self, inspiring others to remember who they are and claim the life of their wildest dreams.

www.briarly.com.au

More from Blue Angel Publishing®

WATER TEMPLE ORACLE

Suzy Cherub
Artwork by Laila Savolainen

Replenish, flourish and flow!

Immerse yourself in the wisdom of eleven sacred water temples and their goddess guardians and emerge revitalised. A beautiful stream of creativity, awareness and consciousness flows from Aphrodite, Mother Ganges, Anuket, and other vessels of sacred knowledge from around the world.

44 cards & 192-page guidebook.
Silver-foil lettering on top box and guidebook cover, packaged in a hardcover box.
ISBN: 978-1-922573-36-0

More from Blue Angel Publishing®

Star Temple Oracle

Suzy Cherub
Artwork by Laila Savolainen

Embody your sacred feminine powers and receive interstellar guidance with this glistening oracle from author, speaker and intuitive coach Suzy Cherub. The ancient wisdom of the Pleiades is weaved together with present-day mysticism to bring you uplifting and relevant insight.

Star Temple Oracle has been birthed to support your learning, creativity, awareness, and growth. Connect with the eternal knowing of the stars and let your intuition flow.

44 cards & 104-page guidebook, packaged in a hardcover box.
ISBN: 978-1-925538-87-8

More from Blue Angel Publishing®

Faery Temple Oracle

Wisdom and Wonder to Empower Your Faery Spirit

Suzy Cherub
Artwork by Christine Karron

With a sprinkle of possibility, a shimmer of starshine and a whisper of wonder, faery magic is ready to ripple through your world, clearing pathways, releasing limitation and imbuing your heart with clarity, purpose and understanding.

---

44 cards & 120-page guidebook, packaged in a hardcover box.
ISBN: 978-0-648746-87-4

More from Blue Angel Publishing®

ANGELIC LIGHTWORK HEALING ORACLE

Healing, Magic and Manifestation with the Archangels

Alana Fairchild
Artwork by Daniel B. Holeman

Generate loving magic for soulful healing and manifestation through the luminous presence of four powerful archangels. Enhance your inner light, reveal your healing path and rejoice in your spiritual awakening through this visionary deck. Complete with 44 healing practices, this beautiful oracle is an invitation to heal and awaken with the support and guidance of the angelic realm.

44 gold-edged cards & 240-page guidebook with card stand, packaged in a hardcover box.
ISBN: 978-1-922573-23-0

More from Blue Angel Publishing®

WHISPERS OF ALOHA

Angela Hartfield
Artwork by Christina DeHoff

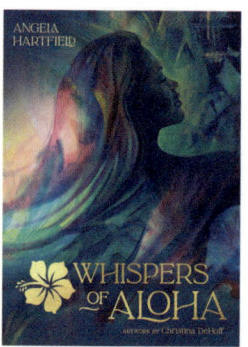

Embrace the bliss, empowerment, and spirit of Aloha through Angela Hartfield's oracular ode to her island home. In her signature style, Angela illuminates the wisdom within the artworks, so they convey personal meaning for detailed and revelatory readings. The lush imagery by Maui-based Christina DeHoff provides a visual connection to the elements, deities, nature, and joys of Hawaii. Revel in glorious inner and outer landscapes, dance where worlds meet, and immerse yourself in wonder as you discover direction, guidance, purpose, and harmony.

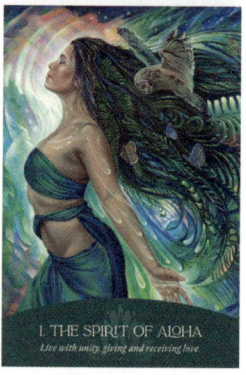

44 cards & 160-page guidebook.
Gold-foil lettering on covers
packaged in a hardcover box.
ISBN: 978-1-922573-46-9

Oracle of the Sacred Horse

Kathy Pike
Artwork by Laurie Prindle

Ride higher planes of harmony and connection

As well as offering honest and supportive responses to your questions, this oracle will deepen your kinship with the horse spirits so you can be enlivened by their freedom, grace, power, and agility — and feel these qualities reawaken in you, unbridled.

41 cards & full-colour 144-page guidebook. Gold-foil lettering on cover, packaged in a hardcover box.
ISBN: 978-1-922573-72-8

For more information on this
or any Blue Angel Publishing® release,
please visit our website at:

www.blueangelonline.com